CONCILIUM

Religion in the Eighties

CONCILIUM

Editorial Directors

General Secretariat: Prins Bernhardstraat 2, 6521 AB Nijmegen, The Netherlands

Concilium 201 (1/1989): Fundamental Theology

CONCILIUM

List of Members

Advisory Committee: Fundamental Theology

1789
THE FRENCH
REVOLUTION
AND THE CHURCH

Edited by
Claude Geffré
and
Jean-Pierre Jossua

T. & T. CLARK LTD
Edinburgh

February 1989
ISBN: 0 567 30081 1

ISSN: 0010-5236

Typeset by C. R. Barber & Partners (Highlands) Ltd, Fort William
Printed by Page Brothers (Norwich) Ltd

Concilium: Published February, April, June, August, October, December.
Subscriptions 1989: UK: £29.95 (including postage and packing); USA: US$49.95
(including air mail postage and packing); Canada: Canadian$64.95 (including air mail
postage and packing); other countries: £29.95 (including postage and packing).

Contents

viii

1789
THE FRENCH REVOLUTION
AND THE CHURCH

Editorial: 1789-1989

WHAT A contrast between the first centenary of the Revolution and the current celebration of the bicentenary! In 1889, the opposition between a republican, secular France and a Catholic, monarchical France was still clearly visible. Today, the situation has become much more complex and it can be said that there is a fairly broadly-based consensus in favour of a less simplistic view of the great event of 1789. This is not only because Catholic historiography has stopped denouncing the satanic character of the Revolution. It is also because contemporary historians, on the basis of a critique of modern totalitarianism, have arrived at a more realistic judgment of the utopia of the Revolution.

Beyond fashionable and opportunistic judgments, it seemed to us that there was room for an issue of *Concilium* which attempts to measure the long-term theological consequences of this event which continues to symbolise the dividing line between a *before* and an *after*. What is involved, in effect, is the never-ending dialogue between the Church and the modern world.

Faced with such a demanding task, we must immediately begin by emphasising the limits of our project. We do not claim to provide a complete historical dossier on the way in which the Church welcomed, or rather refused to welcome, the Revolution. We do not wish, either, to take up again for its own sake the great debate concerning the Church and the rights of man. Our purpose is rather to revive, for today and tomorrow, the so far unrealised possibilities latent in the history of the complex relationship between the Church and the Revolution. And, as will be seen, if a Christian understanding of the Revolution has become possible, it is

3

not so much through drawing up an inventory of the Christian 'themes' of the Revolution as through reflecting on the theme of the Revolution itself as social change and refusal of the inevitability of fate. Our sole aim is, starting from very diverse viewpoints, to enrich a public debate in which the most delicate questions have at least the merit of being asked.

Why did the 1789 Revolution, which symbolised the victory of liberty over all forms of absolutism, encounter such violent hostility from the Roman Catholic Church? Must one speak of the Revolution in terms of a radical break in a long Christian tradition, or see in it an unexpected consequence of the Gospel message? What is the explanation for the inconsistency of the Catholic Church after Vatican II, enthusiastically espousing the doctrine of the rights of man yet not always respecting the 'rights of Christians' within its own institutions? And lastly, can the celebration of the bicentenary also be the celebration of the reconciliation between the revolutionary ideal of '89 and the message of Christian liberty?

In the first part, by singling out a few curious examples from an enormous historical dossier, we have sought to illustrate the complexity of the relationship between Christianity and the Revolution. It seemed important to begin by recalling the contrast between the French and American Revolutions as far as their relationship to Christianity is concerned. Whereas in France the Revolution was the incarnation of hostility towards religion identified with the Catholic Church, in America the Revolution represented rather a form of support for religion and its legitimate pluralism. C. F. Mooney shows how greatly those who framed the American Constitution were concerned to promote a wide degree of religious pluralism. This is why they rejected at the same time any notion of an established religion. For his part, J. Comby recalls the laborious implementation of the famous republican slogan 'Liberty, equality, fraternity' and its practical impact on the life of the Church. The Civil Constitution of the Clergy (12 July 1790) radically reorganised the Church of France. But at the same time it cut that Church in two and led to a break between revolutionary ideals and the Roman Church which was to last until the eve of Vatican II. From another viewpoint, how could one omit the exciting story of that citizen Christian, the Abbé Grégoire? B. Plongeron reminds us what a pioneer he was in the search for a theoretical and practical reconciliation between the rights of man and those of God, between the ideals of the Revolution and those of Christianity. In this bicentenary year, he still remains an exemplary figure worth discovering.

The second part seeks to help us to make progress in the analysis of the causes of the Church's non-acceptance of the Revolution. J. Moltmann reflects on the distance between the enthusiastic welcome given to the idea of revolution by German philosophy (Kant, Hegel, Fichte . . .) and the deliberately anti-revolutionary stance adopted by the Churches, Protestant as well as Catholic. In his opinion, it is only in the search for a new social contract that modern democracies will be able to realise the promises of the French Revolution. G. Cholvy's article helps us to understand the counter-revolutionary attitude of the Church by studying the profound traumas endured by the Christian consciousness. But in fact, as contemporary historiography emphasises ever more clearly, one must not overestimate the role of the Revolution in the de-christianisation of France. Continuity is much more important than the periods of disruption and religion remains firmly one of the pillars of popular culture.

One cannot celebrate the bicentenary of 1789 without reappraising the 'myth' of the French Revolution and the ideology of the rights of man. The aim of J. Comblin's somewhat provocative article is to expose the essentially bourgeois character of the Revolution of 1789; the European bourgeoisie even succeeded in using the rights of man to legitimatise its own power. As a further proof of this, it can be observed that, for want of a bourgeoisie, a revolution equivalent to the French Revolution has always been impossible in Latin America. The ruling elite has hastened to welcome the ideals of 1789, in particular the idea of a state based on legal rights. But in reality, in most South American countries, this is still only a fiction. There is, in any case, one legacy of that 'bourgeois' revolution which Catholicism has always been incapable of thinking out and challenging, that is to say, political and economic liberalism. In the absence of the article which would have been desirable, we offer a review of the particularly stimulating book by the American Michael Novak, *The Spirit of Democratic Capitalism*. Lastly, in an admirably well-documented article, D. Menozzi seeks to reconstruct the framework of thought which was to remain the common heritage of Catholic culture until the advent of Vatican II. The French Revolution is the final outcome of a process which began with the Renaissance and the Protestant Reformation and which continued through the philosophy of the Enlightenment. Thus, for the Roman magisterium, the only adequate response to the historical currents which allowed 1789 to come about, was to rebuild medieval Christendom.

It was appropriate, in the third part, to tackle directly the question of the reception given to the ideals of the Revolution by the present-day Church which, after a long period of hostility, has officially espoused the doctrine of the rights of man. In the first article, which is both very well-documented historically and very courageous, P. Eicher seeks to show the significance of the French Revolution in relation to the Church's exercise of power internally and in its dealings with the world. For all those who are waiting for urgent reforms in the government of the Church, the Revolution remains a parable full of meaning. When Catholics today make the defence of the rights of man an essential requirement of Christianity, are they merely updating a long Christian tradition or are they taking up a 'theme' of the Revolution? And if one takes the Revolution itself as a theme, in what sense may one attribute a 'Christian' character to the theme of the revolutionary changes in society? It is to these fundamental questions that P. Colin attempts to offer an answer, clearly distinguishing between the republican and socialist interpretations of the theme of the Revolution.

No-one can deny the acceptance by the Church after Vatican II of the civil, social and political doctrine of the rights of man. But what is the situation with regard to the Roman Church's internal practice? In a rigorously argued article, B. Quelquejeu examines, with the aid of precise examples, the striking contrast between the Roman Church's present commitment to respect for and promotion of the liberties and rights of man and its failure to recognise the 'rights of Christians'. Such inconsistency must have deep-seated causes. One comes to the conclusion that the rights of man as affirmed by the Roman Church certainly do not coincide at all points with the 'Rights of Man' in the tradition of the French and American Revolutions. Finally, in an issue devoted to the Revolution and the Church, it was impossible to ignore the considerable gap which exists between the revolutionary themes of '89 and the original research of the theologians of liberation. As P. de Charentenay demonstrates, in Latin America the two great agents of the revolutionary process of liberation are the poor and the people of God, from a communal and messianic viewpoint, in which social and religious issues are closely linked.

Such is the hazardous endeavour which we offer to the judgment of the readers of *Concilium,* in the firm conviction that the bicentenary celebrations go well beyond the specific case of France. Two centuries later, the events of 1789 continue to give all Christians cause for reflection. And if today we have a different interpretation of the great revolutionary themes of equality, secularity, democracy, liberty of conscience and religious freedom, this is not only because we are looking at society in a different way, but also because modern theology has not yet finished sounding the depths of the mystery of the Church in the world.

Translated by L. H. Ginn

Claude Geffré
Jean-Pierre Jossua

PART I

Christianity and the French Revolution

Christopher F. Mooney, SJ

Religious Freedom and the American Revolution

WHILE THE larger differences between the American and French Revolutions, in their genesis, goals and accomplishment, are generally well-known, the striking contrast between their impact upon religion has not received the attention it deserves. In France religion tended to be identified with the Catholic Church and this church with the *ancien régime*; hence the French Revolution inevitably symbolised hostility to both. In the American colonies, on the other hand, religion was identified with no single church, much less with the English government, and the American Revolution engendered no hostility at all but rather support for religion. In this article I want to spell out precisely the nature of this support.

There were three stages in the development that took place. The first was social and concerned the general acceptance, long before the Revolution itself, of the fact of religious pluralism. Religious freedom flourished in the colonies, chiefly due to the openness and sparsely settled nature of the country: the non-conformist simply moved away into that vast space where his deviance immediately became orthodoxy. Groups holding divergent and incompatible views on religious questions thus gradually came to co-exist in different parts of the country. As a sense of national community grew, giving birth to political consensus in resistance to Great Britain, disagreement on things religious came to be regarded as less and less important.

The two principal movements in American Christianity at the time, moreover, rationalism and pietism, tended to encourage this growing belief that formal differences in doctrine and worship were not of ultimate importance. Rationalists like Franklin and Jefferson believed that the essentials of any religion could be reduced to a common set of intellectual propositions regarding God, immortality and the life of virtue. Pietists, on the other hand, in the tradition of John Wesley, were convinced that spiritual nourishment had to be found in experience, not in the barren intellectualism of creeds, doctrine and theology. Thus rationalists appealed to the head and pietists to the heart to reach the same conclusion at the very time that, for geographical reasons, many different sects were enjoying relatively peaceful co-existence.[1]

This *de facto* pluralism meant that none of the dominant churches was in a position to press for religious uniformity. Indeed, there was a practical necessity for all of them to connive at religious variety; because no single church could make a successful bid for national establishment, it was to the self-interest of each to be tolerant of all in order to guarantee such toleration for itself. The motivation was thus purely pragmatic; very few church pronouncements at the time articulated any positive ideological thrust for toleration. This *de facto* pluralism likewise made one other conclusion unavoidable: since so many sects, holding very different beliefs, were able to co-exist in peace, it followed that uniformity of religious practice was obviously not essential to the public welfare, something hitherto assumed to be true for centuries by all the countries of Western Europe. It was this last realisation, that religious solidarity was not needed to stabilise the social order, which made it unnecessary, once the new nation was founded, to put the coercive power of the federal government behind the inculcation of religious belief.

This rejection of coercion in favour of persuasion did not mean, however, that government should be indifferent to religion, since from religion came truths essential for public order and stability. The principle meant rather that responsibility for inculcating these truths, thought to be common to every religion, rested with the churches alone, to be carried out in whatever ways individual churches wished, relying upon persuasion. We should note too that this first social stage was in many ways the natural extension into the religious sphere of the eighteenth century's key idea that free consent was the only rational basis for organising civil government.

All the Protestant churches gradually came to accept this ideology for pluralism, reformulating it to fit their respective traditions which originally (with the exception of the Baptists) contained little or no theoretical justification for it. Pluralism was eventually justified as a new outward manifestation of traditional Protestant anti-authoritarianism, fostering anew traditional Protestant virtues of voluntarism and privatism. One far-reaching result of such reformulation was a new organisational form for Protestant churches. They began to think of themselves eventually as 'denominations', groups which neither claimed to be exclusively 'the Church' nor absolutised the peculiarities which distinguished them from other groups. Unlike a 'sect', a 'denomination' recognised itself as a finite witness to the Christian gospel, imperfect in knowledge and authority as well as in practice. Henceforth, it was thought, the federal government could never become involved in any way in the religious sphere without immediately threatening the free church system either by patronising some churches or by coercing all.

This social acceptance of religious pluralism led to the second stage, which was political. Bernard Bailyn has documented with admirable clarity what he calls the 'contagion of liberty' that swept America and infected all areas of colonial life. Indeed, as he says, 'the fear of a comprehensive conspiracy against liberty ... lay at the heart of the Revolution'.[2] It was therefore taken for granted that the purpose of all constitutions in the colonies was to specify and protect inalienable rights and to limit the ordinary actions of government. The suspicion of every type of political power not derived from the people inevitably became a suspicion of ecclesiastical power also, since that too represented a form of coercion, the dominion of some people over others.

All establishments of religion in the various colonies consequently came under fire, both from sectarians who wanted freedom *for* their sects, and from political idealists, inspired by the rationalism of the Enlightenment, who wanted freedom *from* these same sects. The sectarians, also referred to as 'dissenters', were the Baptists (the largest in number and the most vocal) the Quakers, and many Methodists and Presbyterians. They tended to see all government negatively, as mainly coercive in character, and believed in the complete separation of religion as the highest manifestation of their liberty as Christians. The movement's early leaders, Roger Williams and William Penn, created in Rhode Island and Pennsylvania something totally new at the time, colonies without religious establishments. The acute individualism of the Baptists, moreover, as well as their religious impulse of withdrawal, accorded well with the civic individualism of the 'enlightened', and it was, as Bailyn says, 'touched by the magic of the Revolutionary thought' and transformed.[3]

Jefferson and Madison were both 'enlightened', and as such viewed religion instrumentally, as very much a private affair of conscience and opinion, but something nevertheless very useful for the promotion of civic virtue. Jefferson believed that any truths about God and the universe could be known by rational examination of nature alone, without need of any divine revelation, and this conviction he distilled in what he regarded in his writings as second only to the Declaration of Independence, Virginia's 'Act for Establishing Religious Freedom'. Madison, who was influenced by the Anglicism of his youth, and, as a student at Princeton University, much more by the Presbyterian, John Witherspoon, seems to have held beliefs more profound and complex than those of Jefferson, and clearly not as opposed to the concept of revealed religion. Yet he was nevertheless an adamant foe of establishment. Faced with a 1785 proposal in the Virginia House of Delegates for a three pence tax to provide for religion teachers, he wrote his 'Memorial and Remonstrance Against Religious Assessments' that gave his reason for this opposition: establishment had meant coercion in the past, and it was therefore a violation of basic human freedom to require anyone to support a religious undertaking.

The non-involvement of government in religious matters was, therefore, the principle defended by Jefferson and Madison throughout their lives. This they did primarily to protect freedom of conscience. But they both also wanted to promote the freedom of religious practice, in Jefferson's case because he saw that such practice promoted good citizenship, in Madison's case because he also saw it as a bulwark to strengthen religious belief. Hence their principle of separation was not an absolute, all inclusive, prohibition, but could be accommodated on occasion to advance political and perhaps also, for Madison, religious ends.

As governor of Virginia, Jefferson drafted a 'Bill for Appointing Days of Public Fasting and Thanksgiving' (introduced by Madison in the Virginian legislature), that required all ministers to preach on these occasions, and he did not hesitate to invoke 'nature's God' in the Declaration of Independence and in his second inaugural address as President. For his part, Madison raised no constitutional objection in Congress, less than two months after the First Amendment became effective, to government support of a chaplaincy system, and, as President during the war of 1812, he issued four proclamations recommending public days of prayer and fasting, though much later in his life he considered both actions to have been ill-advised.

This effort of Madison to avoid collisions in the religious area appears clearly in *The Federalist Papers*, where in Numbers 10 and 51 he captured perfectly that suspicion of power which, as we saw earlier, was the dominant political ethos of the time. He specifically mentions religion as one of the causes of competing 'factions', groups seeking to advance their narrow private concerns. These factions, he says, are inevitable in a free government, and the aim of a separation of powers in the new constitution should be not to harmonise but to neutralise them, thereby enabling enlightened elected leaders more easily to perceive and promote the common good. In Number 51 Madison finds in religion the analogy for this realistic pluralistic stance. 'In a free government the security for civil rights must be the same as that for religious rights. It consists in the one case in the multiplicity of interests, and in the other in the multiplicity of sects. The degree of security in both cases will depend on the number of interests and sects.'

This combined influence of the sectarians and the 'enlightened' led to the third stage of development, which was legal, namely the enactment in 1789 of the religion clauses of the First Amendment to the United States Constitution. Madison was the one who introduced into the First Congress these guarantees of religious freedom. He proposed two separate amendments, both of which were firmly rooted in the theory of religious pluralism that he had espoused in *The Federalist Papers*.

The first of his proposed amendments was this: 'The civil rights of none shall be abridged on account of religious belief or worship, nor shall any national religion be established, nor shall the full and equal rights of conscience be in any manner, or in any pretext, infringed'. The second read: 'No State shall violate the equal rights of conscience'. Several objections were raised immediately to the effect that these provisions might injure religion. Madison's reply emphasised his double concern to prevent coercion and to encourage a multiplicity of sects. He said 'he apprehended the meaning of the words to be, that Congress should not establish a religion, and enforce the legal observation of it by law, nor compel men to worship God in any manner contrary to their conscience'. He 'believed that the people feared one sect might gain pre-eminence, or two combine together, and establish a religion to which they would compel others to conform'.

After discussion and modification by two committees (Madison was a member of one), the amendments went to the full House of Representatives. Samuel Livermore of New Hampshire moved the following: 'Congress shall make no laws touching religion, or infringing the rights of conscience'. This was again modified by a version proposed by Fisher Ames of Massachusetts, which the House of Representatives finally adopted: 'Congress shall make no law establishing religion, or to prevent the free exercise thereof, or to infringe the rights of conscience'. The House also passed Madison's second amendment regarding the states. In the Senate this second amendment was immediately dropped, no doubt because of suspicion of federal power over the states, and the first House of Representatives amendment was changed again: 'Congress shall make no law establishing articles of faith or a mode of worship, or prohibiting the free exercise of religion'. This revision was apparently not acceptable to the House of Representatives, however. A conference committee of both houses, of which Madison was a member, then produced the final form that we have today: 'Congress shall make no law respecting an establishment of religion, or prohibiting the free exercise thereof'.[4]

We have one action by this first Congress indicating that these clauses relating to religion did not signify total non-involvement of the federal government with things religious. The same legislators who enacted the First Amendment also, with no dissent from Madison, re-adopted in 1789 the Northwest Ordinance of 1787, the third article of which read as follows: 'Religion, morality and knowledge, being necessary to good government and the happiness of mankind, schools and the means of learning shall forever be encouraged'. After citing this bit of evidence, Walter Berns pointedly remarks: 'It is not easy to see how Congress, or a territorial government acting under the authority of Congress, could promote religious and moral education under a Constitution that ... forbade all forms of assistance to religion'.[5] Also, in the course of debating the First Amendment, the first Congress recommended a day of national thanksgiving and prayer. Encouragement of religion in general is evident, finally, in the fact that public taxes at the time were paying for military, legislative and prison chaplains.

Hence we can know what the framers meant by the clauses on religion only up to a point and not beyond. All of them, whether for religious or for civic reasons, wanted the numerous religious bodies to flourish in society in complete freedom. All of them wanted to prohibit a national establishment of religion. All of them wanted to prohibit any intrusion by the federal government into an individual's freedom of conscience, whether this freedom be of a specifically religious nature or not. This broad consensus on general policy, however, was driven by large differences in motivation. To use John Courtney Murray's distinction (though not in a way he would have approved), for some framers the two clauses were simply 'articles of peace', good and prudent lawmaking made socially necessary by the 'contagion of liberty'; for others they were just as surely 'articles of faith', either theological convictions that freedom from government was a religious imperative, or Enlightenment ideologies that such freedom was a natural right.

As for Madison, he may well have wanted Congress to require a greater degree of separation than many members desired. The framers were certainly influenced by his conviction that religious freedom should be limited neither by religious institutions nor by government, and that all such institutions should be denied the support of government power. But we cannot determine the degree of this influence. Beyond this we have only guesswork. Too many minds and motives were at work; too many differences and ambiguities surfaced on secondary issues; too many compromises went into the vagueness and grand simplicity of the text.

We may conclude then, that, at the end of this third stage of development, these clauses on religion of the First Amendment to the US Constitution did not create a new idea, but were rather the legal recognition of an actual state of things which had come to be seen as practically unavoidable. The founders wanted to formulate a principle which would guarantee the participation of all churches in the common social unity of the republic, while at the same time not compromising those distinctive modes of worship and belief proper to each. The First Amendment was therefore conceived to be a legal experiment in the political realm, an effort to strengthen the new nation by excluding from federal government concern all religious differences among its people. At the time it was by no means certain that the experiment would be successful, that is to say, that it would necessarily be conducive to public peace and order.

Writing in 1785, six years before the Amendment's adoption, Jefferson reminded his State of Virginia that the States of Pennsylvania and New York had long had an official policy both of religious freedom and of religious disestablishment. 'The experiment was new and doubtful when they made it', he said. 'It has answered beyond conception. They flourish infinitely. Religion is well supported; of various kinds, indeed, but all good enough; all sufficient to preserve peace and order. . . .' Speaking on this same question in 1808, seventeen years after the Amendment's adoption, Jefferson could say: 'We have solved by fair experiment, the great and interesting question whether freedom of religion is compatible with order in government, and obedience to the laws.'[6] Somewhere, then, within the twenty-three year period between these two statements, the experiment proved to be a success, socially, politically and constitutionally. Religious pluralism finally became acceptable in theory as well as in practice.

Notes

1. Sidney E. Mead, *The Lively Experiment: The Shaping of Christianity in America* (New York 1963), pp. 5–15; 24–27.

2. Bernard Bailyn, *The Ideological Origins of the American Revolution* (Cambridge 1967).

3. *Ibid.*, p. 271.

4. The texts are from the *Annals of the Congress of the United States*, cited by Michael J. Malbin, *Religion and Politics: The Intentions of the Authors of the First Amendment* (Washington 1978), pp. 6–14.

5. Walter Berns, *The First Amendment and the Future of American Democracy* (Chicago 1985), p. 8.

6. Saul K. Padover (ed.), *The Complete Jefferson* (New York 1943), pp. 538, 676.

Jean Comby

Liberty, Equality, Fraternity: Principles for a Nation and for a Church

FOR MANY of our contemporaries the republican motto 'Liberty, equality, fraternity' constitutes the most concise summary of the heritage of the French Revolution. In reality, it was not until 1848 that the three words were formally written into the French Constitution. Certainly, from the start of the 1789 Revolution the three words were often loosely associated. Sometimes fraternity was missing. The order of listing varied. To this triad were linked unity, indivisibility or even death as alternatives. Some, obsessed with chronological logic or ideological systemisation, would claim to find in the history of the Revolution three successive phases: the liberty phase, the equality phase and finally the fraternity phase; after which we would return to the starting point with Bonaparte. Things are not as simple as that. The Revolution sees the triumph of the word. But putting words into practice is a different matter. The tenor of the words varies within the same period. For some, equality has merely a legal sense, others give it a social and economic meaning. The meaning that some attribute to fraternity is given by others to equality. Moreover, the most sublime words may have been completely misinterpreted: 'Liberty, how many crimes are committed in your name!'

We are not concerned here with a history of the Revolution nor with revolutionary vocabulary. We are simply trying to highlight some significant moments in the proclamation and realisation of revolutionary ideals. More especially, we will see their effect on the life of the Church and of christians: how were the three principles accepted or rejected? How did they transform ecclesiastical structures?[1]

17

1.   The Nation and the Church regenerated by the Rights of Man

When he summoned the States General to resolve the financial problems of the kingdom, Louis XVI provoked the rise of the aspirations which until then had been contained. These were expressed in the registers of grievances. Although not always coherent, the claims may have been inspired by the spirit of the Enlightenment, sought the end of absolutism and the arbitrary nature of royal government, the establishment of a constitution, and equality before the law, justice and taxation. The clerics demanded a fairer distribution of ecclesiastical wealth and claimed a greater degree of consideration vis-à-vis the bishops. All came from the nobility. We can recognise in this traces of the Gallican, Richerist and Jansenist currents which had been filtering through the French Church for more than a century.

At the end of June 1789, when, under pressure from the Third Estate and then from the clerics representing the king, the king asked representatives of the three orders to sit together as a National Assembly, the Revolution really began: the orders disappeared, representatives were equal. The abolition of privileges (on the night of 4 August 1789) and the *Declaration of the rights of man and citizen* (26 August 1789) founded a new society on the two principles of liberty and equality: 'Men are born and remain free and equal in rights. . . .' In the name of this liberty, it was the responsibility of the citizens bearing national sovereignty to define the law equal for all. This liberty applied to political and religious opinions, written and spoken: 'Every citizen may speak, write and print freely'. Respect for the rights of man should 'be directed to the well-being of all', but with the exception of 'property, an inviolable and sacred right', there is no mention of social or economic rights.

On these principles, the Constituent Assembly reorganised France from top to bottom. Religious discrimination disappeared; Protestants and Jews became complete citizens. At every geographical level (canton, district, département, region) and in all sectors (administration, justice, the Church), citizens would elect their representatives freely. Liberty was complete in the organisation of work and in the economy (Law *Le Chapelier*, 4 June 1791). Of course, they did not go as far as possible with these principles, particularly in respect of equality. In spite of Condorcet's favourable view,[2] it was scarcely thinkable that women should have the right to vote. Elsewhere the right to vote and eligibility were reserved for citizens who were liable for a tax determined by the members of the Constituent Assembly. Several, including Robespierre and the Abbé Grégoire, protested against this discrimination which divided the French into active and passive citizens. In spite of several proposals, slavery was retained in the colonies. The Law *Le Chapelier*, which suppressed guilds, at the same time forbade workers to group together for the defence of their interests.

The liberty and equality claimed by the Declaration of 1789 and the Constitution of 1791 reflected the conceptions and the interests of the bourgeoisie of the time. However, from the start of the Revolution other aspirations had surfaced, appearing sporadically in the writings, the celebrations and some of the social achievements of the Constituent and Legislative Assemblies. The anniversary of the Federation of 14 July 1790, commemorating the taking of the Bastille, glorified fraternity, which became the object of an oath: 'After the oath, it was a touching sight to see the citizen soldiers throw themselves into each other's arms with promises of liberty, equality and fraternity'.[3] This fraternity could also have a fighting dimension. By excluding enemies of the Revolution, it sought to confront the threats which faced it. It demanded the suppression of discrimination between active and passive citizens.

Many members of the Constituent Assembly could see the potential danger of political and social egalitarianism. Nonetheless, the Constitution of 1791 proposed the setting up of social and scholastic institutions: 'A general institution of public assistance will be created to look after abandoned children, the poor infirm, and to provide work for the able-bodied poor who would not be able to find it. A system of public education will be established and organised, common to all citizens, free as far as essential education for all men is concerned. . . . National holidays will be instituted to preserve the memory of the French Revolution, to maintain fraternity among the citizens and bind them to the Constitution, the fatherland and the law.'[4]

The Mendicancy Committee of the National Assembly, founded in January 1790, engaged in great activity: statistical enquiries, administration of hospitals, creation of poor houses and public workhouses, etc. One of the most famous members of the Committee, La Rochefoucauld-Liancourt, spoke in very strong terms: 'As every man has the right to subsistence, society must provide subsistence for any of its members who may lack it, and this helpful aid must not be regarded as a kindness. . . . This duty must not be demeaned either by the name or the character of the charity: national assistance is an inviolable and sacred debt for society.'[5] For him, poverty ran counter to the principles of liberty and equality. It is true that some members of the committee only envisaged the struggle against poverty in the perspective of the maintenance of order. Elsewhere, the decrees concerning the struggle against poverty, though relatively numerous, were not very effective. The social situation was often made worse by the dismantling of the old charitable system.

From the earliest days of the Revolution, the Church in France was caught up in the general process of national regeneration. The clergy, as an order, disappeared. It renounced its privileges on the night of 4 August: seignorial rights and tithes. It surrendered its wealth to the nation on 2 November 1789, Equality and national solidarity had truly concrete consequences for the Church. Although these arrangements were not willingly accepted by all, they did not provoke serious opposition, particularly as the priests were assured of a reasonable salary. The consequences of liberty were less enthusiastically welcomed. Many saw in religious liberty a relativisation of the place of Catholicism in France. There followed several attempts, which came to nothing, to pass a vote on a text safeguarding the privileged place of the Catholic Church (Dom Gerle, April 1790). It was in the name of liberty that the members of the Constituent Assembly banned solemn vows and thus suppressed the contemplative orders (13 February 1790). Monks and nuns, however, remained free to leave their establishments or stay there. This measure did not provoke strong feelings. The same could not be said in the case of the Civil Constitution of the Clergy (12 July 1790) which radically reorganised the Church in France. In the Church, as in the rest of the nation, sovereignty came from the people: bishops and priests would be elected by the same electors who appointed the administrative and legal authorities. The principles of the Declaration of Rights were combined with the old Gallican and richerist claims. Religious officials had to swear 'to be faithful to the nation, the law and the king and to preserve the Constitution decreed by the National Assembly' (27 November 1790). The Civil Constitution and the compulsory oath broke the Church in two.

Some accepted the new ecclesiastical organisation, judging that the revolutionary principles had their roots in Christianity: 'Let us worship God as sovereign author of the revolution that makes us free . . . The true system of Catholicism is that of universal liberty. . . . Examine in itself this system of pure fraternity, and see, if tyrannies had not altered it, to what a perfect state of liberty, equality and unity it would have brought the organisation of society. . . . What is the Catholic Church? It is the society of brothers under the authority of legitimate pastors. What are legitimate pastors? Those whom the brothers have freely elected. . . . There are no poor in such a fraternal society; there are only equals.'[6] But the majority of bishops and a large number of priests considered the Civil Constitution unacceptable because it ignored the authority of the Pope over bishops and local churches. Also, Pope Pius VI, in condemning the Civil Constitution (March–April 1791) at one stroke also condemned all the revolutionary principles and in particular those rights of man which were the cornerstones of this new Church: religious freedom, freedom of conscience, freedom of the press and the equality of all men. All these rights were opposed to the will of the Creator. Yet the bishops who affirmed their opposition to the Civil Constitution dissociated themselves from the Pope in his irrevocable condemnation of liberty and equality: 'We have sought to establish the true domination of public liberty within a hereditary monarchy and we have recognised without difficulty that natural equality which excludes no citizen from the places to which he may be called by Providence through his talents and his virtues. Political liberty may be extended or restricted according to the different forms of government; and we have believed that our opinions were free, like those of all citizens on these more or less broad questions which God himself declares as open to human debate.'[7] In spite of these important subtleties, the Roman Church appeared from that time on as the great adversary of revolutionary regeneration, and it gradually fell prey to persecution.

2.   Liberty, Equality, Fraternity or death

The Constitution of the Year I (24 June 1793) voted by the Convention reveals an evolution of the founding principles of the Revolution. The Declaration of Rights which forms a prelude to it was enriched in comparison with the Declaration of 1789. The basic rights are still 'equality, liberty, security, property'. But equality comes before liberty. The status of servant or slave is not recognised. And above all, we see appearing the right to subsistence by work or by public assistance; the right to education; and finally, the right to revolt. In the Constitution itself, universal suffrage is introduced for men, the advocates of votes for women not yet having managed to impose their wish. Now it is necessary for a foreigner seeking French citizenship to have only one year's residence in France, instead of five previously.

Through conviction, and also under pressure from the people of Paris who expressed themselves in clubs and popular societies, the members of the Convention drew up an important programme of social legislation, at least until Thermidor (July 1794). Slavery in the colonies was abolished (4 February 1794). The most ambitious social law was the one which provided for the opening of a Great Book of National Charity (11 May 1794). In this book were to be written the names of all citizens with a right to subsistence: disabled farmers, old and infirm craftsmen, mothers and widows. It was social security before the term existed: health-insurance, state pension scheme, family allowances . . . Unfortunately, as one historian said, 'the Great Book was scarcely opened.' The financial difficulties were too great to be able to satisfy the demands. The Convention legislated for primary education in the most democratic sense (December 1793). The law provided for compulsory education, free for all children. Areas with between 400 and 1,500 inhabitants had to have a school. Freedom of teaching remained. In fact, the law was actually applied in fewer than 10 per cent of the districts.

All these democratic measures were taken during the dramatic period of war with Europe, civil war in the west and south-east, and the power struggle which led to the successive elimination of the principal leaders of the Convention and the popular societies. Aid for the poor was often subordinate to a certificate of patriotism, and death became an alternative to the great principles: 'Unity, fraternity, indivisibility of the Republic, liberty or death.'[8]

The period from September 1792 to July 1794 was also the period of struggle against the recalcitrant priests, then of de-christianisation which struck just as much at the constitutional Church. In the upheaval, the representatives of the Church scarcely had the time to express their opinions on the democratic trend. Grégoire, bishop of Loir-et-Cher, intervened in the Committee of Public Education. For him, the democratisation of teaching was linked to the struggle against local dialects and to the standardisation of the French language. A liturgy in French would aid the progress of the language: 'The abolition of coarse idioms will be even nearer if, as I hope, 20 million Catholics decide that they will no longer speak to God without knowing what they are saying to Him, but will celebrate the divine office in the vernacular.'[9] There were also those 'red priests' who adopted extreme positions in favour of the people. Fauchet, bishop of Calvados, proclaimed that every man has a right to the land. Jacques Roux, who came from Saintes to Paris, vicar at Saint-Nicolas des Champs, made himself the violent and demagogic spokesman for the *enragés*, who demanded measures in favour of the very poor: 'Liberty is only a vain phantom when one class of men can starve another with impunity. Equality is only a vain phantom when the rich man, through monopoly, exercises the right of life and death over his fellow man.'[10] The Gospel had doubtless inspired them at first, but they scarcely appeared at that time as representatives of the Church!

3.   The tide turns

With the elimination of Robespierre (27 July 1794), the Thermidoreans tried to stem if not stop the democratic tide and to consolidate the advantages gained by the bourgeoisie since 1789. These concerns passed into the Constitution of the Year III (22 August 1795). The retreat was marked in comparison with 1793 and even 1789. The Declaration of Rights was presented in the driest manner. The right to work, the right to aid, the right to education all disappeared. No longer were freedom of opinion and freedom of the press made issues, though they were discreetly mentioned at the end of the Constitution. The only social right retained was the abolition of slavery.

This social disengagement was shown in the body of legislation of the Directory. Primary schooling was no longer a concern. Only the central departmental schools which were to provide secondary education for the children of the bourgeoisie were important. In the area of assistance, the idea of national solidarity was shelved. The Directory endeavoured to transfer the responsibility for national assistance to local communities and private charity. A law of 7 October 1796 organised 'civil poor-houses'. This meant that hospitals had to find their own means of funding. They were given back their former properties. They could collect revenue from bequests, taxes from entertainments or gifts from individuals. The administrations took back the former nuns who had been dismissed at the time of de-christianisation. The situation of hospitals, not exactly flourishing in itself, was made even worse by the need to accommodate the war-wounded. The welfare offices should have distributed aid to people's homes but they could not begin the task, so great was the poverty. Private charitable associations reappeared.

The longing for an egalitarian society remained. It was behind the conspiracy of the equals organised by Gracchus Babeuf (March–May 1796). Babeuf envisaged the suppression of property and the sharing of resources, and a democracy conducted in basic assemblies. The arrest of these conspirators enabled the Directory to eliminate its last opponents on the left. But, to confront a royalist upsurge, references to the old revolutionary ideal seemed ineffective, since state employees were compelled to take 'an oath of hatred of royalty and anarchy' (1796–1797).

The great principles which became blurred in political life took refuge in religion. The appeasement following Thermidor led Grégoire to claim freedom of worship which was recognised on 21 February 1795. The constitutional Church, now separated from the State and seeking merely to establish a Gallican Church, regrouped around Grégoire. It aimed to re-unify believers and to promote the revolutionary ideals from the religious angle: 'We pride ourselves on being the ministers of a religion whose moral code is composed of all the useful virtues of society. . . . whose distinctive character is brotherly equality. . . . The Gospel states that men are brothers. The Gospel hallows the principles of equality and liberty.'[11] The Roman

Catholics were not very sensitive to these words, all the more so since theophilanthropy, a substitute religion supported by the Directory, also sought to associate religious language with political language: 'As a sign of union and equality, let us, in the name of all opinions, exchange the holy kiss of brotherhood'.[12]

The constitutional Church operated in a highly democratic way. This meant that not only did it take account of the revolutionary principles but it returned to the ideas of the early Church. The electoral principle is rooted in the Acts of the Apostles (the election of Matthias). The episcopal council which the bishop had to consult before taking a decision recalls the ancient presbyterium. From 1795, the constitutional bishops who had formed a united committee of bishops placed the emphasis on their collegiality. In each diocese, the presbytery, taken from the body of priests which we would today call the council of the presbyterium, supported the bishop or administered any diocese without a bishop. The 'Gallican' Church called two national councils in 1797 to 1801. To prepare for them, diocesan synods were convened in which believers could take part. The councils were very insistent in their demands that the liturgy should be intelligible to the whole of the Christian people by the use of French in the sacraments. Without making too much of the decisions of a Church which was badly received by many French people, it should be stressed that it was anticipating in several points the transformations which would only see the light of day with the Second Vatican Council.[13]

Conclusion

When Bonaparte took power on the 18 Brumaire (9 November 1799), the majority of French people were relieved to find that 'security' which had been present in all the declarations of rights of the different revolutionary constitutions. But from them on, Bonaparte's constitutions would contain no more declarations of rights. It is true that the consuls stated in the text which introduced the Constitution of the Year VIII (15 December 1799): 'The Constitution is founded ... on the inviolable rights of property, equality and liberty. The powers instituted by it will be strong and stable, as they must be to guarantee the rights of citizens and the interests of the State. Citizens, the Revolution is bound to the principles which began it: it is finished.'[14]

Slavery was re-established in the colonies. A complicated system of election neutralised the popular forces. The poor were even poorer than in 1789. The inequality of fortunes increased. Only a bourgeoisie, which at the right time had been able to acquire national wealth or profit from supplying victorious armies, benefited from these ten years of revolution. The Catholics, happy to find religious peace, would henceforth view revolutionary principles as satanic and would, for a time, put up with a Church under the iron rule of the First Consul, soon to become Emperor. The latter counted on religious principles to neutralise those other principles of liberty, equality and fraternity which had inspired such great hopes in the hearts of the people in 1789.

And yet it is not in 1800 nor in 1815 that stock must be taken of 1789. It is today. The generations which have followed the Revolution up to our own times have not wished liberty, equality and fraternity to be empty words. Throughout the nineteenth and twentieth centuries, the struggles for democracy, for human rights, for a fairer economic organisation have given the republican slogan a meaning which it did not have at the start. And Christians—some had thought of it in 1789—have realised since then that the three words had a truly evangelical resonance.

Translated by Barry Mackay

Notes

1. It is inappropriate here to provide a bibliography on the history of the Revolution and the Church. We only indicate some recent works which have particularly influenced this study: Alan Forrest, *The French Revolution and the Poor* (Oxford 1981) (French translation, *La Révolution française et les Pauvres* (Paris 1986)); Marcel David, *Fraternité et Révolution française* (Paris 1987); Jacques Sole, *La Révolution en questions* (Paris 1988).

2. *Sur l'admission de la femme au droit de cité*, July 1790.

3. M. David, *op. cit.*, p. 68.

4. First title of the Constitution of 1791; *cf. Les Constitutions de la France depuis 1789*, introduced by J. Godechot (Paris 1979).

5. A. Forrest, *op. cit.*, p. 58 (French ed.).

6. Claude Fauchet, 'Sermon sur l'accord de la religion et de la liberté' (Paris, 4 February 1791) in Migne, *Collection intégrale et universelle des orateurs sacrés* (Paris 1855) vol. 66, cols. 159–174.

7. 'Lettre des évêques députés à l'Assemblée nationale, en réponse au Bref du pape du 10 mars 1791' (Paris, 3 May 1791); quoted in H. Leclercq, *L'Eglise constitutionnelle* (Paris 1934), pp. 371–372.

8. M. David, *op. cit.*, p. 181.

9. 'Sur la nécessité et les moyens d'anéantir les patois et d'universaliser la langue française' (28 May 1794).

10. Quoted in P. Christophe, *1789, Les prêtres dans la Révolution* (Paris 1986), p. 162.

11. M. David, *op. cit.*, pp. 246–247.

12. M. David, *op. cit.*, p. 252.

13. *Cf.* B. Plongeron, 'L'exercice de la démocratie dans l'Eglise constitutionnelle de France (1790–1801)', *Concilium* 77 (1972), pp. 125–132.

14. *Constitutions de la France*, *op. cit.*, p. 162.

Bernard Plongeron

The Birth of a Republican Christianity (1789–1801): Abbé Grégoire

IN THE generation of the 'men of liberty', the man who will be known forever as 'Abbé Grégoire' (with a street named after him in Paris), though he was a constitutional bishop, occupies a special place. One reason is that he remained serenely to his death the model citizen-priest, indifferent to all the political cliques, even under Napoleon. He could write in his memoirs, 'I am classed among those who, since they cannot be bought, must be crushed'. The other, and more important, reason is his passion for the universal. Unlike the utopians of the Enlightenment, Henri-Baptiste Grégoire went into action at an early date for the great causes of humanity, the freedom of the Jews, the emancipation of the blacks (especially in Haiti), the fate of the poor and humiliated. For him this was part of a great vision of a confederation of scientists, philosophers and theologians from all over Europe who would work to celebrate the achievements of Christianity since its origins (which almost succeeded in 1796 when the Société de Philosophie Chrétienne came into being) and even to reunite the separated churches (*Mémoire sur les moyens de parvenir à la réunion des églises grecques et latines*, 1 June 1814).

This young man from Lorraine, born on 4 December 1750 at Vého near Lunéville was to live an exemplary life in obedience to prophetic intuitions. But it was a life so complex that he has not yet received the great biography he deserves, despite many partial studies,[1] and above all paradoxical enough for this benefactor of humanity to become the most vilified man in France, notably in the election campaign of 1819, when, as the candidate of the liberals, Grégoire was elected deputy for Isère. Branded as a regicide, despite the evidence to the contrary, Deputy Grégoire was ruled not invalidly elected but unworthy to take his seat—an event without precedent which shocked the firmest anti-clericals, starting with Stendhal, who called him 'the most honest man in France'.

Because it is impossible to describe, even in broad outline, Abbé Grégoire's life and writings (427 titles in the official catalogues and thousands of letters),[2] I would like to offer a basis of interpretation. What fascinated Grégoire's friends and enraged his opponents was a man committed to and involved in a logic which he built up patiently by research and enquiry on the spot in France and in Europe, through acquaintance with all the leading personalities of the century, in politics the church and intellectual life.

This logic consisted essentially of three stages corresponding to key moments in Grégoire's life, and often in that of France. Under the *ancien régime* he launched an intellectual assault on all despotisms, to which he owes his reputation—very much exaggerated—as a Jansenist. The success of his first battles would normally have made him a militant partisan of the declaration of human rights. However, because he found it incomplete without a declaration of 'divine rights', he was forced to go further, to a symbiosis of the Christian and the citizen. He found this embodied first in the 'national religion', the ideal of 1789, but intended to perfect it through the creation of a 'republican Christianity' (after the abolition of the monarchy on 10 August 1789). This was for him the perfect expression of his political theology, which he believed he could live out within the constitutional Church, of which he became in effect the moral leader after the Terror. As though crushed by his own logic, Grégoire was to figure in the pantheon of the Revolution's losers, albeit having sown a Christian democrat posterity which was to take almost a century to become established and did not always realise the debt it owed to its initiator.

1. A champion of the universal against particular despotisms

For Grégoire, an acute observer and prodigious and cosmopolitan reader, Lorraine was a testing ground for all the movements of the Enlightenment. Coming from as far afield as England (via Holland) and Italy, from the Jansenists of the French 'interior' to the Febronianism of the Rhine, in Lorraine they mingled and clashed and in the end produced a showcase of the Christian *Aufklärung*, which was to be the blueprint for all his pastoral and political activity.

Grégoire discovered the need for a critique of despotism, first from the Abbé Cherrier, the parish priest of Embermesnil whom he succeeded in 1782 and who taught him the grammar of Port-Royal, Racine and the scriptures, and later at the university of Nancy and the major seminary of Metz. At Metz he had among his teachers the Lazarist A. Lamourette, the future constitutional bishop of Rhône-et-Loire, theological adviser to Mirabeau and possibly the inventor of the concept of 'Christian democracy'.[3] He did not acquire it in the version of the 'philosophers', who made it the *Leitmotiv* of the Enlightenment, and still less from the series of theological commentaries from Lessing to Kant, whose 'dark metaphysics' (sic) revolted him, as it had all the classical French thinkers of his generation; but much more from the idea of the *ecclesia antiquior*, so dear to every Catholic *Aufklärer*.

Only a doctrinal and 'historical' return to the theological, liturgical and ecclesiastical practices of the church of the apostolic age and the first councils would put an end to the degeneration of a church, which had, by its abuses of power, excessive material wealth and political compromises, engendered and maintained all the despotisms which had allowed superstitions to proliferate by keeping the people in ignorance. To free people from cultural oppression and cultural childhood is to raise them to the combined dignity of Christian and citizen of the state, under the symbol of the 'rational' worship which St Paul recommends to the Romans (Rom. 12). This was a foundation text of the Catholic Enlightenment, because the *rationabile obsequium* opened the way for a new religious anthropology, appropriate to the political model of a church of 'responsible Christians' appealing to the common priesthood of the baptised. The phrase appears explicitly in the address to the Constituent Assembly on 27 November 1790 by the lawyer-canonist Camus, future first archivist of France.[4] It was inspired by this theological Augustinianism cultivated by all the adherents of the Western European Enlightenment and practised in exemplary fashion at Port-Royal.

Was this Jansenism? In becoming the first historian of the 'monastery', Grégoire showed how and why he intended to widen the answer by situating it within broader perspectives. No doubt he was attracted by the model of the *ecclesia antiquior*, lived, he believed, by the religious women and the Gentlemen of Port-Royal: a humble life combined with charity to the poor and the children of the 'little schools'; a piety hostile to the lavishness of the baroque, at the service of an ecclesial 'memory' purified by an understanding of the scriptures and a critical study of tradition. There is no doubt that Port-Royal captivated him, but no longer as a theologico-political 'party', a coterie, rather as the locus of the universal, of Christianity in the process of renewal, a process which included the democratic structures of the community of the Gentlemen. However, this locus of an ecclesiological universal was also the symbol of martyrdom at the hands of politico-religious despotism. This despotism showed itself in the absolutism of Louis XIV, for whom he could not find words harsh enough: 'For long years under his rule France had been covered by the laurels of victory and the tatters of poverty. He died laden with the eulogies of the poets and the hatred of the people.' This despotism, he continued, justified the priests who took the oath (*Ruines de Port-Royal*, 1801).

For a moment, as is well-known, he won national notoriety when the Academy of Metz honoured his *Essai sur la régénération physique, morale et politique des Juifs* (1788), by which he sought to restore dignity to this group which Christian states had proscribed. This was the explanation of his election to the States-General: 'I had come to the Assembly resolved to plead the cause of the Jews.' The significant term 'regeneration' has often been misunderstood. 'Grégoire's idea was to make the Jews full citizens, and so 'regenerate', that is, able to enter as persons into the enlarged Christian community, and not to defend the particular characteristics of the Jewish 'nation'. It is a paradox of this champion of universalism that he was never, in the religious field, a promoter of ecumenism, even in relation to his protestant friends. He remained far too 'Tridetine' to make that qualitative leap.

2. A militant partisan of the 1789 Declaration of Rights

As the star of the meetings of the Third Estate with a clergy majority which transformed the States-General into a national Constituent Assembly, Grégoire was naturally expected to be one of the staunchest defenders of the *Declaration of Rights*. However, he chose to join the drafting committee and not the ecclesiastical committee, one of whose tasks was to present the Civil Constitution of the Clergy.

Was this the infallible logic of an attitude adopted under the *ancien régime* which was to lead him to an opportunistic republicanism? Grégoire was a man of extreme complexity, captured with rare precision by the man who was to be his companion to his death, Deputy Thibeaudeau. He retained an exact recollection of his friend at the height of his fame:

'Though a priest to the tips of his fingers and the bottom of his soul, he was one of the deputies for whom I had the most liking and respect. He had so much good faith, candour, courage and devotion as a patriot and revolutionary ... He made no loud proclamations of his republicanism, but gave every appearance of being one and was so reputed. Without being exactly an orator, he spoke with boldness, warmth and facility.'

It should be added that his interventions were feared for their weight of references. Whatever the subject, from religion to agriculture via the universality of the French language or the establishment of a Conservatory of Arts and Crafts, one is overwhelmed by the abundance and precision of the references and notes in the most insignificant petition and in every one of his more than a thousand speeches.

An enemy of all labels—a characteristic which was to be both his good fortune and his peril under the Terror—this man of inflexible principles, never sufficiently anxious about being understood, still less 'caressed', as he kept repeating, had studied history, and especially church history, closely enough to discover that every great fracture is preceded by an insurrection of consciousness. What is a tortured or offended consciousness? What cry, under the pain of oppression, shoots up from consciousness into the face of an indifferent universe? How far may a consciousness go, and what means may it use, when threatened with annihilation by political, religious and ideological systems? The questions which obsessed Grégoire are extraordinarily modern, and he himself was first an 'avenger' of all the voiceless before himself being deprived of a voice and falling victim to his own demands.

To tell the truth, except for the Jansenist crisis—which is revealing—Grégoire prefers the word 'heart', so full of resonance in the century of the Enlightenment, to 'consciousness', but the identification is quite clear to him. The human 'heart' has an innate need for freedom, justice and happiness, an incessant dialectical trilogy. This need is 'consecrated' by religion. Grégoire was thus unable to accept, unlike other deputies, that human beings were the source of their rights (Kant).

Contrary to a widely held belief, the birth of the Declaration was painful and long. No less than fifteen drafts were defended more or less well by 56 speakers between 9 July and 26 August 1789. At the beginning of August the Assembly began to tackle the prickly subject of the preamble to the Declaration. Once again it returned to the American model of 1776—to find that God was explicitly mentioned in it. How would the French Declaration deal with this issue?

Abbé Grégoire immediately swept aside the hesitations of his colleagues and, as so often, transformed the underlying question. Not only should God be mentioned—the last concession to be made to him—but also logic decreed that if mention was to be made of the inalienable rights of the human being, 'we should speak of Him from whom he holds them and who has imprinted duties on him, God!' And at that memorable sitting of 18 August the deputy for Lorraine demanded that the Declaration of Human Rights should be accompanied by a declaration of human duties to God, since 'Man was not thrown at random on to the corner of the earth which he inhabits; everything refers this secondary creature to a primary cause', since he himself was a part of the consciousness of the God of the universe. It was not until the constitution of the Year III (1795) that there was any mention of human 'duties'.

Though a precursor of an anthropology of the 'national religion', Grégoire nonetheless sent a firm denial to Rome when it saw fit to denounce the 'unbridled freedom' (*licencia* being substituted for *libertas*) contained in the 'detestable philosophy of human rights' (Brief *Quod Aliquantum* of March 1791). Anxious to develop against all odds the implications of the 'national religion', Grégoire multiplied, to good effect, his interventions in 1789–90 in favour of the Jews and 'people of colour', who came to hear of him as far away as the Caribbean. He also saved social peace by presiding for 72 hours over the Constituent Assembly besieged by a crowd agitated after the taking of the Bastille. He quelled the tribunes and restored the confidence of his colleagues: 'Let us teach this people which surrounds us that the terror is none of our doing . . . We will save our newborn freedom, had we to be buried under the ruins of this chamber.' Who then noticed, through the unanimous applause, that this impenitent liberal was peremptorily declaring that nothing would ever make him confuse demagogic pressures with the political morality which should be the pride of a democracy, above all at its birth?

3. Opportunities and limits of a republican Christianity after 1792

This political morality was to be found only in the principles of a 'national religion'. This was even the title of a successful book by Claude Fauchet, curate of Saint-Roch in Paris and future constitutional bishop of Calvados. This leader of the progressive wing of the Constituent Assembly expanded on the key theme accepted by all in 1789: the Christian will be the best citizen because Catholicism, under the existing constitution, is and will remain the 'dominant' religion. In this reaffirmation of the Catholic-dominated Christian society, how could the law be atheist? 'Good people, it's impossible.' The hypothesis seemed so absurd that another patriotic enthusiast, the Carthusian Dom Gerle (immortalised in David's painting *le Serment du Jeu de Paume*) proposed in 1790 that the National Assembly should simply declare Catholicism the state religion, without completely realising that this would once more put a question mark against the civil rights of Protestants and Jews.

Nonetheless the prestige of a 'national religion' occupied people's minds and reassured them during the apotheosis of the festival of the Federation on 14 July 1790. Two days before, on 12 July, the Civil Constitution of the Clergy had been proclaimed with the King's approval. For the moment, and despite the publication of the articles of this questionable document, the 5000–6000 *fédérés* massed in the Champs de Mars, including some 300 priests and chaplains of the National Guard (many of whom were later to become dissidents), seemed less than shocked by a Civil Constitution of the Clergy so firmly anchored in the ideal of the citizen Christian. On 27 December, a few days before the first clergy were due to take the oath, when the battle over the appropriateness of this civic gesture was becoming more bitter, Grégoire went to the podium of the Assembly and expressed a conviction which he was to retain to his deathbed. After mature consideration, he insisted that he 'saw nothing in the Civil Constitution of the Clergy which can harm the sacred truths which we have to believe and teach. It would be a slander on the National Assembly to attribute to it a desire to wield the censer. Never has it sought to interfere in the slightest with dogma, the hierarchy or the spiritual authority of the church'. In his view, taking the oath was a 'patriotic duty which will bring peace to the kingdom and consolidate the unity between pastors and flocks'. His speech led 62 deputies to take the oath, among them seven bishops.

According to the most recent calculations, some 52–55 per cent of the French clergy supported the constitutional Church before the papal condemnations of March–April 1791, and despite wide regional variations. There was therefore a real possibility of organising a French church which would reconcile religion and revolution. Grégoire seemed best placed to be the soul of this national renewal. An adulatory press was already envisaging him as constitutional bishop of Paris. Though he had not offered himself as a candidate, the departments of Sarthe and Loir-et-Cher elected him at the same time by large majorities. He chose Loir-et-Cher with that suspicious lucidity he retained all his life about the honours pressed on him. This man of liberty, this priest burning with pastoral zeal, did not want to be a bishop. 'St Augustine,' he wrote, 'had taught me that to be a bishop is the heaviest burden. My reluctance was overcome only by the imperious voice of religion calling for new pastors and the order of those who directed my soul.' Consistent with his principles, on the day after his episcopal ordination he sent a letter of communion to the Pope:

> 'Most holy father, I have received canonical institution and have been duly consecrated. I profess, in mind and heart the Catholic, apostolic and Roman religion. I declare that I am and will always be, with the help of God united in faith and communion with you as the successor of St Peter with the primacy of honour and jurisdiction in the church of Jesus Christ.'

Disillusionment, bitterness and then open disappointment during the sequence of events from September 1791 to 1792 overwhelmed the democratic utopianism which Grégoire still cherished, forcing him to harden his tone and to reformulate his version of republican Christianity for the situation after Thermidor. In the pastoral field building the organisation of the constitutional Church was a painful process. No-one had foreseen either the hostility of the local administrative authorities with regard to the funding of the new parochial and diocesan structures (few seminaries were functioning properly in the spring of 1792) or the poor quality of many pastors, including bishops bullied by their episcopal councils under the pretext of democratic collaboration. Grégoire was to learn this to his cost in Loir-et-Cher. A bishop out of duty, he put all his energies into three pastoral visits, something his predecessor, Mgr de Théminés, who had left the Chambéry in 1791, had not done for 13 years. He was to be seen everywhere, especially in 1792, when, ineligible for the Legislative Assembly, his presence in Paris was less necessary. He preached 52 times in 40 days, arousing the enthusiasm of the religious communities themselves. Unfortunately he was recalled to Paris as a member of the Convention and was to have his trust betrayed by incompetent or corrupt episcopal vicars. His hatred of married priest dates from then. In politics, he discovered from his vantage point in Blois the gulf opened among the French people by the constitutional oath, particularly in Vendée. He blamed the King, whom he regarded after his flight and arrest at Varennes (21 June) as nothing but a perjurer, a traitor to the Civil Constitution of the Clergy which he had approved solemnly, a traitor to 'the country in danger' and so to the national sovereignty in the name of which he had declared war 'on Bohemia and Hungary' (20 April 1792). With his consistent attitude to despotism, Grégoire allowed himself to be carried away by extravagant language against the monarchy: 'What matters the flight of a perjurer we can very well do without? He will swear anything and keep nothing'.

Grégoire was proud to begin his new term by getting the Convention to proclaim, on 21 September 1792, that 'the monarchy is abolished in France'. Had he not declared in March in his cathedral at Blois, 'Anyone who does not love the republic is a bad citizen and consequently a bad Christian'? What he had not foreseen was the organic law of secularisation of 20 September, which provided for the creation of civil status in place of the church registers and, above all, the authorisation of divorce and the marriage of priests. Defying Grégoire's logic, the republic was showing him that the law could, and even had to be, atheist.

How was the ideal of the citizen Christian henceforth to be preserved? With the great majority of the patriotic bishops, Grégoire immediately and clearly came out in favour of a Christian polity: their pastoral letters condemned civil divorce and priestly marriage absolutely. It was now, at the end of 1792, that there began the extreme tension between theology and politics: for the first time Catholic leaders were confronted with the massive fact of a secularisation which some authors today applaud as the modernising effect of the revolution. Not for a single instant did Grégoire, any more than his fellow bishops, consider attempting a 'theology' of this revolutionary secularisation. Intransigent on dogmas and sacraments, more 'post-Tridentine' than one would have expected considering their intellectual and theological formation, they refused to yield to the temptation offered, namely to eliminate the Christian in favour of the pure citizen with a civic morality. After Thermidor the bishops who had escaped the Terror went on to develop a political critique of the ideas of liberty and equality, 'prostituted by corrupt regimes' and to stress the distinctiveness of the evangelical virtues. Grégoire likewise termed 'schools of the devil' (the phrase is from 1791) the republican institutes designed to produce atheist citizens.[5]

Grégoire saw militant atheism on the benches of the Convention. At the height of the de-christianising persecution which led priests to resign their priesthood the bishop of Blois sat in the Convention, at the risk of his life, in skull-cap and purple stockings. On 17 Brumaire (7 November 1793), when Bishop Gobel and his episcopal vicars came to resign their priestly functions, he declared: 'Catholic by conviction and sentiment, priest by choice, I was chosen by the people to be a bishop; but it is neither from them nor from you that I hold my mission.'

With these proud and courageous words he withdrew to the Committee of Public Instruction, where he continued his original work, fostered by the logic which inspired his whole life: the development of France as the locus of the universal of republicanism, through the humanitarian, cultural and economic liberation of national resources. This is the thread running through his most famous contributions: against slavery, which culminated in the anticipatory decree of 16 Pluviôse of Year II (4 February 1794) on the abolition of slavery 'without compensation or redemption'; 'on the need and the methods for destroying dialects and universalising the use of the French language' (6 June); on the industrial renewal of France, no longer to be enslaved to England or Germany in these economic fields, by the creation of a Conservatory of Arts and Crafts (3 October), which would recognise women's work; on the protection of the artistic, scientific and cultural heritage; and through three great reports *On vandalism*, a word he created.

Thus, in the darkest days of a France which had every reason to despair of its civilising mission, Grégoire, in contrast, saw the need for laying practical foundations for a 'social art' capable of concentrating all republican energies—and leaving it to a religious renewal to sacralise it.

1795 and 1796 were years propitious to the construction of a republican Christianity, purged by the de-christianising persecution. With three other bishops, former members of the Convention like himself who had been released from the prisons to which they had been consigned in Year II, he reorganised the constitutional Church while getting the Thermidorian Convention to pass a Declaration of the Rights of People (23 April) which is a unique illustration of the political philosophy of the renewed structures of the post-Thermidor constitutional Church. I have previously described the practical applications of this exercise of democracy.[6] Here it must suffice to note briefly that it was rooted in the theological principles of ecclesiastical consensus, unity of faith, unity of priesthood and unity of communion, embodied in the procedure of election and the functioning of elected bodies with the participation of lay people according to their degree of 'priesthood'. The two national councils of 1797 and 1801 inaugurated parliamentary procedures which were not to be adopted in the church until Vatican II. Similarly one should stress the modernity of some of these conciliar decrees, such as the one on the liturgy in French, where Grégoire showed a boldness too prophetic for the liking of his colleagues, being prepared, if necessary, to welcome 'the Chinese tom-tom' into Catholic services!

Besides the odd whim and even the need to draw on the rich treasury of Gallican traditions, there was the desire to make the constitutional Church a model of political liberty.

'The true foundations of political liberty are in the Gospel because the Gospel ceaselessly reminds human beings that, coming from the same stock, they form a single family; that between them there exists, not *a sort of kinship* ... but a consanguinity whose ties are indestructible;

constantly the Gospel inculcates in human beings the spirit of charity and feelings of fraternity. . . .'

And if the French Church achieved this model of freedom, why should it not be exportable, first to the rest of the Catholic world and then to all the other Christian families? This is the source of Grégoire's *Projet de réunion de l'Eglise russe à l'Eglise latine* (12 October 1799).

After the traumas of the Revolution this appetite for a universal rediscovered by Christianity was more widespread than is usually thought in the Europe of the Directory, on the threshold of the nineteenth century, the century of the 'springtime of nations' and of industrial take-off. Not only was it quickly muzzled by the conservative movements which revived thanks to the Europe of the Holy Alliance, but it also degenerated into a politicisation which transformed those scientists, philosophers and theologians who had invented a world humanism into sectarian 'liberals'.

Grégoire always refused to be such a sectarian; he was the perpetual loser of the Revolution as it was strangled by the 'despotic' regimes of the Empire and the Restoration. Rather than let himself be bought by the honours and stipends pressed upon him, he preferred to withdraw from public life to establish himself as the moral authority of Europe and Africa. He devoted himself by incessant journeys and a vast correspondence to his two eternal causes, the emancipation of the Jews and the struggle for the liberation of the blacks.

4. Grégoire's revolutionary modernity and his posterity

Since no-one is a prophet in their own country, it is not surprising to find Grégoire better known and more revered from the nineteenth century to our own day among European Jews and the blacks. In 1825 two representatives of the Republic of Haiti came to negotiate with Charles X French recognition of Haiti's independence. They were forbidden to go and see Grégoire. But they met him secretly, 'after dark', and fell at his feet. On the announcement of his death, on 28 May 1831, Santo Domingo went into public mourning. In Haiti a salvo was fired every quarter of an hour to the memory of 'the friend of people of all colours', as he had called himself, and all the black clergy joined in celebrating a solemn liturgy.

For French Catholics his enduring reputation was of a 'Jacobin' and a 'regicide'. So the Protestant Guizot, the liberal who, with the constitutional monarchy, achieved a compromise between the legitimists and the heirs of '89, in 1830 refused to restore Grégoire either to the Chamber of Peers or to the Institute. Lamennais, who might have been thought his spiritual heir, could not stand him, and Victor Hugo gave his support to the filthy campaign provoked by his 'scandalous' election in Isère in 1819 (*Les Misérables*, Pléïade edition, 1951, p. 1533).

The hatred he attracted was equal to the respect compelled by his intellectual and moral virtues. It also made it easier to steal his ideas. He knew and advised countless 'young' advocates of 'social Catholicism': Joseph Droz and Baron de Gérando, whose first books were directly inspired by the philanthropic ideas and the remedies for pauperism he found in many of Grégoire's minor works. Buchez was fascinated by the great man—until he took it into his head to rehabilitate Robespierre, when the doors of the little apartment in the Rue du Cherche-Midi were abruptly closed to him. The good Abbé Augustin Sénac copied entire passages of *L'Influence du christianisme . . . sur l'abolition de l'esclavage* (1813) and *Sur la condition des femmes* (1821) in his successful book *Le Christianisme considéré dans ses rapports avec la civilisation moderne* (1st edn. 1837), but how could he pay his debt to the 'heretic'? And what should one say of the Christian democrat, Abbé Maret, when in 1847–48 he dealt in his Sorbonne lectures with 'the constitution of the Church and its relations with democracy'?

Convinced in his lifetime only of the loyalties which are earned, the 'former bishop of Blois', as he persisted in signing himself, had his last days darkened by an odious blackmail in which he was forced to retract his constitutional oath in return for the sacraments of the church, but a mass of young people carried his coffin to Montparnasse cemetery. 20,000 workers and students gave him a triumphal procession.

Grégoire, youth of the church and of the world? Why not, even if it was not until the bicentenary of his birth, in 1950, that one Ho-Chi-Minh, president of the Democratic Republic of Vietnam, paid official tribute, during important cultural events, to 'the apostle of the liberty of peoples'?

In this bicentenary of the French Revolution 'Abbé' Grégoire remains to be discovered through his logic of the citizen Christian, which he lived out passionately in the front line of the men of liberty—of God and in God.

Translated by Francis McDonagh

Notes

1. B. Plongeron, 'Grégoire, Henri-Baptiste', *Dict. Hist. et Géo. Eccleés.*, fasc. 126 (1987), cols. 60–71

2. *Oeuvres de l'Abbé Grégoire* (Paris 1977), 14 vols. Preface by Albert Soboul, 1st collected edition of 143 texts published between 1788 and 1831 in a chronological and thematic arrangement.

3. H. Maier, *Revolution und Kirche. Studien zur Frühgeschichte der Christlichen Demokratie, 1789–1850* (Freiburg in Br. 1959).

4. B. Plongeron, 'Recherches sur l'Aufklärung catholique en Europe occidentale (1770–1830)', *Rev. Hist. Modern et Contemporaine* 16 (1969), pp. 555–605; 'Was ist katholische Aufklärung?', *Katholische Aufklärung und Josephinismus* (Vienna 1979), pp. 11–56.

5. B. Plongeron, *Théologie et Politique au siècle des Lumières 1770–1820*, vol. III, 'Combats revolutionnaires pour une théologie de la sécularisation 1790–1804' (Geneva 1973), pp. 121–183.

6. B. Plongeron, 'The practice of democracy in the constitutional Church in France 1790–1801', *Concilium* 77 (1972) pp. 122–131.

PART II

Reception and Non-reception of the Revolution by the Church

Jürgen Moltmann

Revolution, Religion and the Future: German Reactions

1. The modern era: a new beginning and its contradictions

THE PARIS events of 1789 were hailed in the various states of Germany with messianic enthusiasm by some, while by others they were hated with an apocalyptic terror. But both groups immediately recognised that the French Revolution meant the dawn of 'a new epoch in the history of the world', as Goethe put in on 20 September 1792, after the cannonade of Valmy. The *ancien régime* collapsed, in France first of all, later in the different German states as well; and a new democratic era began, first in France, and from 1848 in Germany too. This was the age of the bourgeois world, and it lasted until the Bolshevik revolution in Russia, in 1917.

The other side of the political revolution, however, was the industrial one that followed. The world of the great industrial areas came into being, the world of new mass cities, the proletariat, European economic imperialism, and the exploitation of nature through human domination. In the twentieth century Europe's political hegemony destroyed itself in two world wars. But the scientific and technological civilisation which it had created spread inexorably, and became global.

Yet today, all over the world, this civilisation finds itself entangled in at least three deadly contradictions.

1. It has produced the misery of 'the third world'.
2. It is driving the earth towards ecological catastrophe through its progressive destruction of nature.

3. It is threatening its own survival through the system of nuclear deterrents, by which it aims to secure its own safety.

In the period leading up to March 1848, German philosophers and poets imagined that with the French Revolution a new time had dawned. Two hundred years later this 'new time' has turned into something very like the 'end-time' of humanity, an era in which at any moment the end of the human race can be brought about by human beings themselves. So if we look back to 1789 from the perspective of 1989, what we see is not unequivocal. It is ambiguous. We are left with mixed feelings. The revolution was never completed. But what form will the completion take?

2. French practice and German theory

Two hundred years ago, the Germans looked on fascinated at the events in France. But looking on was in fact all that they did. They did not achieve anything comparable themselves. Consequently, the political revolution in France was answered in Germany by an intellectual one. One of the first people to spark this off was Kant, with his transcendental philosophy of subjectivity. The great philosophical school of German idealism—Kant, Fichte and Hegel—may therefore be interpreted as the German theory of the French Revolution.[1] So powerful was the impact of events. But in Germany, revolutionary theory was where things stopped. The theory did not lead on to praxis. It was Karl Marx who for the first time brought Hegel's theory of revolution down to earth and made it practical through and through.

Let us look at the events of those early days. When the first news from Paris arrived in Germany, devout Protestants in Württemberg who were waiting for the coming of the kingdom of God, sent an emissary to Paris, in order to find out for certain what was happening. He never came back. But 'the revolutionary wish to bring about the kingdom of God is the salient point of all progressive education, and the beginning of modern history', declared Friedrich Schlegel. And this is important for the German Enlightenment. It was eschatologically orientated. 'The philosophers have their millenarianism too', wrote Kant.[2] In 1791 the theological students at Tübingen university were carried away by the spirit of liberty: Hegel, Schelling and Hölderlin planted a Jacobin cap on the maypole, and danced round it to the sound of the Marseillaise. Terrified, the Duke of Württemberg exhorted them to hear reason. In 1798, talking about the French Revolution, Kant wrote: 'A phenomenon like this can never again be forgotten, because it reveals a disposition and a capacity in human nature for betterment, a capacity which no politician could have thought out for himself from the previous course of events.' Drawing on Thomist sacramental theology, he interpreted the revolution as a 'historical sign' of humanity: it is a sign of remembrance, a sign of hope, and a sign of the presence in the human race of a trend towards the good. That is to say, men and women had emigrated from a self-inflicted tutelage towards the independent and public use of their own reason.[3]

Hegel described the same phenomenon more emphatically: 'Never as long as the sun had shone in the firmament and the planets had revolved round it, had it been perceived that man stands on his head—that his existence centres in his ideas—and that it is there that he forms reality. Anaxagoras was the first to say that the *nous* [the intellect] governs the world; but only now has man come to recognise that thought should govern spiritual reality. And this was indeed a glorious sunrise.'[4]

Fichte related his philosophical system even more directly to the French Revolution: 'My system is freedom's first system. Just as that nation is striking off mankind's outward fetters, so my system strikes off the fetters of things in themselves, of outward influence, and as its first principle sets up man as an independent being.'[5]

The Idealist philosophers saw the ideas of the Enlightenment at work in the French Revolution: *human rights* and human dignity, *democracy* as the constitution of liberty, *reason* as the means whereby to build a free and humane world. All in all, the French Revolution meant the humane emancipation of human beings from their multifarious dependencies and alienations. They recognised in the political revolution the dawn of 'the age of history'. Ever since 1789 'revolution [has become] the identifying mark of our age in world history', said Julius Friedrich Stahl. The future is no longer determined by the past. Traditions no longer legitimise the orders of state and society. The world of men and women has ceased to take its bearings from the cosmic orders of nature. Through the industrial revolution, people have been put in a position to construct their own world according to their own wishes and ideas. Through the political revolution, political rule has ceased to be legitimised by religion; its legitimation is now popular sovereignty. Through both revolutions, human beings have become the determining subjects of their own history. And modern society and the modern state must be rationally organised for this purpose.

But if people become the masters of their own history, they can also dig their own graves. As freedom grows, danger grows with it. In order to keep this danger at bay, men and woman seek for a transcendent support. If this human history of humanity is not to end in chaos, it must take its bearings from a history that is wider, more comprehensive—the divine history of the absolute mind (Hegel), the natural history of evolution (Darwin), or the objective laws of dialectical materialism (Marx and Engels). Although the great thinkers of the nineteenth century thought in terms of the great paradigm 'History', nearly all of them were aware that 'history' is merely another name for 'crisis', and that crisis is simply another word for 'revolution'. History is a ceaseless crisis, and crisis is the 'permanent revolution'.[6] Consequently every mental and political effort was made to discover the historical laws of revolution, to master the social laws of society, and to enforce particular blueprints for the future. Life in history is life in permanent crisis and perpetual new decision. The goal of the new social sciences of Saint-Simon and Auguste Comte was therefore '*terminer la révolution*'—to end the revolution. The popular revolutionary movement can be mastered by sociological knowledge and sociological techniques.[7] So 'to end history' by way of the transition from the revolutionary era to an era made possible by bureaucracy—an epoch '*post-histoire*'—was on the agenda from 1789 onwards, together with revolution itself: from the theocracy of earlier times by way of modern democracy to post-modern technocracy.

3. Anti-revolutionary apocalyptic in religion

When the ideals of the French Revolution were betrayed in the Jacobin terror, and when Napoleon, on France's behalf, made his bid for world supremacy, the initial German jubilation over French liberty soon switched over into an apocalyptic 'terror of the negative' over this 'fury of extinction' (Hegel's phrase).[8] It was the Christian churches above all which saw the Antichrist on the way and which—in the fall of Europe as it had been—conjured up the final struggle of Gog and Magog. *The anti-revolutionary option* came into being in the Catholic and Protestant churches—an option which has endured to the present day. The churches saw a future for religion and Christendom only in 'the Holy Alliance' of Austria, Prussia and Russia against Napoleon. Later on they developed emphatically anti-revolutionary, conservative political ecclesiologies. In the different German states, the Protestant churches hallowed as a religious patriotism the national consciousness that had grown up during the war of liberation against Napoleon (1813): 'For God, king and country.'

Let us look at the testimonies of the time. 'All revolutions are contrary to the kingdom of God', proclaimed the German revivalist theologian Gottfried Menken.[9] In 1831 August Vilmar, a conservative theologian who is still influential even today, termed the revolution 'the abominable monster from the abyss': the revolutionary spirit is the denial of all the higher divine order, and turns people into beasts who merely follow their instincts. The revolution and its children—democracy, emancipation, equality before the law, rationalism and liberalism—are signs of the approaching end of the world. The Antichrist is raising his head, and those who belong to him know 'neither God nor prince, neither order nor law, and they are hence proceeding with all their might to destroy Christianity.'[10]

Julius Friedrich Stahl, the influential Protestant theologian and Prussian churchman and politician, interpreted the signs of revolution with the same apocalyptic solemnity: because the French Revolution is anti-Christian, only Christianity is in a position to heal the nations from 'the sickness of revolution'. With this revolution we have entered upon 'the apocalyptic era': the principle of popular sovereignty as the absolute 'principle of evil'. This revolution cannot therefore be fought with compromises. Nor can it be overcome through a political 'constitutional act'. The only power capable of overcoming revolution is Christianity.

Abraham Kuyper interpreted the storm signals of revolution in exactly the same way. Kuyper was a Reformed theologian, the leader of the Dutch Anti-revolutionary Party and for years prime minister of the Netherlands. For him the quintessence of the French Revolution was the anarchist slogan 'ni Dieu—ni maître' (neither God nor master). He saw this popular sovereignty as the denial of all divine and divinely appointed authority in state and family. So for him atheism led logically to anarchy and the destruction of morals. 'Modernism' and 'Christianity' must fight one another to the end. The struggle between them is itself already the beginning of the end of the world. Kuyper lauded 'Calvinism' as 'the only defence for the Protestant nations that can stand its ground against the modernism that is invading them and flooding over them', for in Calvinism men and women humbly bow the knee before God, but raise their heads proudly towards their fellow men. In modernism, on the other hand, people clench their fists towards God and humiliate themselves before their fellow men. *Reformation against Revolution* is the title of his most influential book.[11] Kuyper's spirit is still alive today in the Boer religion of South Africa, the only difference being that there modernism has been replaced by Communism, and the Bolshevik revolution has taken the place of its French predecessor.

The political apocalyptic of 'the religious right' in the United States (*e.g.* Jerry Falwell)[12] also goes back to the basic anti-revolutionary, apocalyptic option taken up by the churches in the nineteenth century: the French Revolution was the beginning of the end of the world, the Bolshevik revolution leads right into it, and a nuclear 'Armageddon' will in the near future bring about the end itself. Absurd though these notions about the end-time may seem, they are dangerous to the highest degree, and even today show something of the long-term effect of the French Revolution on its opponents.

4. Religion, revolution and the covenant for life

The vision of hope for 'liberty, equality and fraternity' can be betrayed and repressed, but 'it can never again be forgotten', now that it has taken root in the hearts of the oppressed. Anyone who declares that this liberty is a human right can never deny it to anyone at all. So this vision of hope still exerts its influence today, and beyond our own time, in the struggle of oppressed peoples to liberate themselves from European imperialism and in the struggle for freedom of the poor and those who are without rights in all the different societies. The cultural movement for the liberation of women from patriarchy and male industrialism, and the ecological movement for the liberation of nature from human exploitation and annihilation, show how influential these ideas still are, and how far they still cast ever new ripples.

But the anti-revolutionary reaction still makes itself felt too, in *the authoritarian principle* 'God, king (or governmental power) and country (or family)'. In many countries today, the ruling classes are building up authoritarian regimes which they legitimise through the ideology of 'national security'. They are misusing religion by turning it into an ally against the revolution of the people, making out that this revolution is something Godless and anarchical. What they hope for is not a world of justice and peace for everybody, but the decisive apocalyptic battle between Catholicism and socialism (Donoso Cortes) or between Christ and Antichrist (Julius Friedrich Stahl), or between 'the free world' and 'the realm of evil'. Because in the *ancien régime* the churches allied themselves with feudalism, the revolutionary liberty of the people was bound to be justified and fought for only in anti-clerical and atheistic terms. And because the popular political revolution and the proletarian revolution of the workers were atheistic, the churches and their theologians were forced into the conservative camp. The rise of democracy in politics, the development of liberalism and socialism in economics, the growth of scientific and technological rationalism, and the awareness of freedom among ever new classes of people—all these things therefore came up against the suspicion of the clerics and the incomprehension of the theologians.

It was only when the bourgeois age was drawing to a close in western Europe, in the middle of the twentieth century, that churches and theologians hesitantly began to adopt a positive attitude to the developments of the modern mind and spirit which had grown up out of the French Revolution. Vatican II is the great signal for the 'actualisation' of the gospel of freedom in and through the Catholic church. The ecumenical movement is the corresponding sign in the non-Roman Catholic churches. Political theology, the theology of revolution and liberation theology, feminist theology and ecological theology are all new working drafts in our generation which are designed to overcome the fateful and fundamental anti-revolutionary, conservative and apocalyptic option in Christianity; and their purpose is no longer merely *to react* to the development of the modern mind and spirit, but *to run ahead of it*, carrying the light of hope.[13]

This is all the more important, since developments in the modern world have led to such enormous contradictions that today the future of humanity itself is called in question. Faith in progress has given way to fear of the future. Consequently faith in God must save hope for humanity, and liberate it from both hybris and resignation, for perseverance. The real ways out of the danger are neither escapism into the 'post-modern age', nor the gentle seduction of the New Age. Humanity cannot be saved either by capitalism, or by socialism as it really exists; for both of them deepen the social and ecological perils of this world, and are not solutions; they are part of the problem. But a new historic alliance between socialists and Christians, a positive mediation between reason and religion, faith in God and human freedom, would be the presupposition for resolving the conflict between revolution and religion which has existed ever since 1789.

The unsolved and unsolvable problems of the revolutionary hope for humanity is not liberty. It is not even equality. It is the mediation of the two through the *solidarity* which at the time of the French Revolution was called, so biblically and so humanistically, 'fraternity'—brotherhood; although this equally means the sisterhood of women, and the sister and brotherhood of women and men.

Which form of human community protects and effects both liberty and equality, the self-fulfilment of individuals and the mutual recognition and acceptance of people who are different? I believe that this can only be brought about by *a co-operative reform* of modern society 'from below'. The theological and political concept that is relevant here is the concept of *covenant*. This concept moulds the form of God's people in the Old Testament and in the New. It has also put its impress on the constitutional history of the modern democracies which are based on popular sovereignty. In the covenant, men and woman are both free and dependable. Their covenant is the realisation of their mutuality, both in their need and in their abilities. Political covenants in the form of alliances also give effect to international dependencies, even between different social systems. Finally, only a new covenant between human culture and the life of the earth will be able to ensure the survival of both. The covenant of free and equal men and women, drawn from all the different nations, cultures and religions, can 'complete' the French Revolution, because it will fulfil its hope.

Translated by Margaret Kohl

Notes

1. J. Ritter, *Hegel und die französische Revolution* (Cologne 1957).
2. I. Kant, *Das Ende aller Dinge* (1794), *Werke*, ed. W. Weischedel (Darmstadt 1964) VI, pp. 175ff.
3. I. Kant, *Der Streit der Fakultäten* (1798), *Werke, op. cit.* VI, p. 361.
4. G. W. F. Hegel, *Vorlesungen über die Philosophie der Weltgeschichte, Werke*, ed. H. Glockner (Stuttgart 1927–40) XI, p. 557 (ET *Lectures on the Philosophy of History*, trans. J. Sibree, Dover and New York, 1956).
5. J. G. Fichte, *Briefwechsel*, ed. H. Schulz (Leipzig 1925) I, pp. 349f.
6. R. Koselleck, *Kritik und Krise. Ein Beitrag zur Pathogenese der bürgerlichen Welt* (Frankfurt 1959).
7. J. L. Talmon, *Political Messianism. The romantic phase* (New York 1960).
8. G. W. F. Hegel, *Phänomenologie des Geistes* (1807), *Werke, op. cit.* III: 'Die absolute Freiheit und der Schrecken' (ET *The Phenomenology of Mind*, trans. J. B. Baillie, New York 1967; *Hegel's Phenomenology of Spirit*, trans. A. V. Miller, Oxford, 1977).
9. *Cf.* R. Strunk, *Politische Ekklesiologie im Zeitalter der Revolution* (Munich and Mainz, 1971) pp. 102ff.; J. Moltmann, *The Church in the Power of the Spirit*, trans. Margaret Kohl (London and New York 1977) pp. 41ff.
10. A. Vilmar, *Kirche und Welt* (Gütersloh 1872).
11. Kuyper's book was based on the Stone lectures, given in Princeton N.J., and was first published under the title *Calvinism* (New York 1899; reprinted Grand Rapids 1931).
12. G. Fackre, *The Religious Right and Christian Faith* (Grand Rapids 1982).
13. *Cf.* J. Moltmann, *Was ist heute Theologie? Zwei Beiträge zu ihrer Vergegenwärtigung*, Questiones disputatae 114 (Freiburg 1988).

Gérard Cholvy

Revolution and the Church: Breaks and Continuity

THE FRENCH Revolution, quite apart from its reverberations throughout the world and the universal Church, had a fundamental effect on the history of French Catholicism. Within a few years, the Church experienced the collapse of its structures, the dispersal of its divided and proscribed priests, and the persecution of the faithful. A series of setbacks sparked off the crisis.

—The setback represented by the civil constitution of the clergy inspired by Rousseau, Gallicanism and political Jansenism: that is, a constitution for a national church on the lines of the Church of England, or of the Lutheran and Calvinist churches of the German-speaking and Scandinavian countries, and one absolutely contrary to Roman tradition.

—The setback consisting of attempts to establish an official cult of the Supreme Being in Year II, and of the Decadal cult under the Directory.

—The setback of the first separation in 1795.

This collapse of the Church inflicted a deep wound on the Christian consciousness in Europe: one which was to plague it throughout the nineteenth century. It is impossible to understand the counter-revolutionary attitude in the Church without also in some way understanding the extent of the trauma inflicted on it. It was so great that this account must needs be restricted to Roman Catholicism.

Contemporaries felt that there had been a complete break. It is appropriate to look at its religious aspects and to emphasise the point that one reason for this feeling, which was still universally experienced at the time of the first centenary in 1889, is to be attributed to the methodology of positivist historians.

As the second centenary dawns, historians tend on the contrary to minimise the event, or at least not to keep it within the traditional bounds of the decade 1789–1799. Instead they tend to stress the permanent features and continuity, in short to relativise the era, because they have become aware of the dimensions of a greater field within which it seemingly has to be located, which is tantamount to a vital shift in historiography. What is more, having tried to relate the French experience to the Chinese cultural revolution, they ask us to acknowledge the appropriateness of their researches.[1]

1. Breaks

A break appeared and proved permanent at the institutional level. The first threshold of laicisation in France was 20 September 1792 and had to do with civil status. A second break lasted a long time and its consequences were felt more deeply. This was the ratification of the rights of the state in education.[2] Though the Revolution through lack of time merely proffered some theories and managed to destroy a system of education in which the Church had intervened at every level, it was Napoleon who established the University (1806) and showed that he intended to set up an educational monopoly. The second threshold of laicisation was crossed in 1882 with the law regarding public secular primary education. In the spirit of Ferry and the Republicans, it was very much a question of 'moulding a new man' in accordance with revolutionary ideals. But in this area, after a conflict of constant vicissitudes between 1815 and 1984, 'real freedoms' (as in the Anglo-American tradition) eventually prevailed over the 'abstract freedom' which had emerged from the Revolution.

—1833: freedom of primary eduction;
—1850: freedom of secondary education;
—1875: freedom of higher education;
—1959: the 'loi Debré' instituted the contractual system.

It is no less true that the separation between secular education and religion determined under the Revolution caused a break with biblical culture in France the effects of which were to be felt much later, mainly during the major cultural changes of the 1960s. The secularisation of the environment and the disappearance of what we might nowadays call the Church's 'visibility' more or less permanently affected the towns more than the countryside, where the Church with its bell was still a point of reference.

Bill-posting during the 1981 presidential elections showed the extent to which it remained symbolic when the need was felt. In 1790 a town like Chartres contained, for 13,000 souls, more than 50 places of worship, six religious houses, and countless statues of our Lady. Solemn processions were held there. Yet the number of buildings secularised was considerable: 332 chapels were destroyed. There, as elsewhere, religious houses were turned into a gaol, the central school (then a lycée), a prefect's residence and offices, a court or barracks, or a factory. Street names were changed; crosses and shrines were destroyed. Even though worship was re-established, in general the religious restoration of the nineteenth century had little in common with the old order of things. In this area, moreover, the really decisive breaks occurred in the 1960s.

The disappearance or thinning out of religious communities for men or women was felt in the towns for a generation at least. The most extreme feature of this break, the marriage of nuns, nevertheless amounted to no more than 0·6 per cent of the total, that is, 318 cases out of 55,000. Far fewer gave as a reason their lack of a 'vocation' from the start (70; that is, about 0·1 per cent), which makes one wary of taking at face value the fate of Diderot's character in *La Religieuse*.[3] We know, however, to what extent progress in this respect in the nineteenth century considerably surpassed the conditions of the eighteenth.[4]

Louis Pérouas and Paul d'Hollender usefully distinguish between a definitive break, a provisional break, a mere interruption and slow erosion.[5] In a geographical catchment area almost co-extensive with the entire country there was a definitive break in respect of men's Easter duties. Nevertheless, in regard to the rural districts of Limoges, 'we have to ask whether the majority of men really performed their Easter duties before 1789'. The scant data available prompts some commentators to ask if they did, or at least casts some doubt on a supposedly unanimous male observance. This is all the more necessary since nineteenth-century clergy were understandably prone to idealise the pre-revolutionary situation, as a time when, if we are to believe the Bishop of Limoges in 1806, 'all one had to do was keep things going', whereas 'nowadays you have to be a missionary'.

When we remember that the bishop came from an area of Toulouse where the majority undoubtedly made their Easter communion, the statement is questionable. The later restoration work made, so it seems, scarcely any lasting impression in the Limoges area. Of course the generation question is important. Poorly instructed people of the problematical period gradually replaced those Catholics who had received regular instruction until 1793. Certainly the recovery in the number of men performing Easter duties in many areas did not occur until the 1840s, or even later.[6] It is also certain that the rising trend included a majority of men only where the break had been merely transitory, in reconstituted Christian communities. The supposedly unanimous rural Christianity around 1815 rarely corresponded to any reality, as recent research has shown for the Trabes, Strasbourg and Metz dioceses.[7]

In most cases, the break was only temporary as far as civil marriages were concerned. Not all marriages contracted during the problematical period were rehabilitated. The main difficulty was that the couple had to go to confession first. In any case, civil marriages during the period of interrupted worship did not signify a desire to break with the Church. The children of such couples were almost always baptized. From 1810 couples who wished to be married rarely appeared only before the mayor.

With a few exceptions, the use of Republican first names was also temporary, which shows the failure of this extraordinary measure (even the Soviet Revolution did not try it); it involved a changed calendar and the replacement of Sunday with the *décadi*. A survey of 53 communes in the South, from Valence to Perpignan, showed that even in the Year II the number of people choosing Republican names was very scant indeed, with the notable exception of the town of Montpellier. There is no really decisive explanation for this: neither the size of the town nor its functions, nor the presence of Protestants, nor even its 'liberal' reputation in the nineteenth century. 'Blue' towns like Béziers, Carcassone or Perpignan were scarcely implicated. Here a more highly-nuanced analysis is indispensable: that is one which makes distinctions between first names indicating a break or compromise, and those which are inconclusive (the last-mentioned being very numerous among girls), legitimate and illegitimate births, and foundlings, who received their first names from the civil official. Where vast numbers of Republican first names were attributed to people, the results of the survey tend to argue against the spontaneity theory. With a rate of 100 per cent in Floreal of Year II, and 96 per cent in Messidor, there is no doubt that pressure was applied at Montpellier.[8]

Are we to suppose that the interruption of instruction in Christian doctrine was equally transient, and preparation for First Communion too? The restoration of catechisms was often an enforced result of the sheer pressure of population from the end of the Directory, yet it was rather difficult because of the continuous reduction in the number of people who could teach. Raymond Dartevelle has shown for the Alpine dioceses of Gap and Embrun how much this break was resented. On the other hand, it is probable that the Anne-Marie Javouheys or Marie Riviers, fervent catechists who must stand for so many others whose names are unknown, were unable, unless there was a veritable missionary gridwork as in the Lyons region, to re-establish a network. Perhaps the grid was not so well established before the Revolution as was thought to be the case.[9]

The celebration of Sunday Mass was, it seems, merely interrupted. In rural Limoges everything goes to show that there was a general and rapid recovery of worship in 1795, and overall in 1803, and therefore that the process of de-christianisation was arrested at this level, though absences became more frequent among the gentry: 'They say that going to Mass would mean putting themselves on the same level as the dregs of the people', as a country priest of the Rheims region wrote to Grégoire in 1795. We have reason to be much less positive about the observance of Sunday as a day of rest, even when we know how many people resisted the *décadi*.

The final sign of a break is a form of 'slow erosion'. With regard to the rules on abstention and fasting in Lent, there is nothing to show that there was not a partial return to former practices with the reinforcement of the neo-rigorist ascendancy until about 1840.

And so the religious break does not seem to have been so very radical, whatever minority rate may be established and whatever conclusions are drawn from that. Contemporaries and positivist historians thought differently. The quest for 'the historical facts', the non-replicable, is not directed to the statistics of religious observance. Naturally we know most about the behaviour of social elites. Indifference to statistics is conducive to elevating as an 'example' what is often far from 'exemplary'. Contemporaries were often struck by the existence of stubborn pockets, such as the priests who remained unreconciled after the Concordat and tended to associate with one another. Through their family connections and civil positions, many of them were close to the bourgeois dynasties which had acquired church property and whose interests tended to support their convictions. Among the posts offered them, we may note teaching in colleges and in the army, which were hotbeds of anti-clericalism during the first few decades of the nineteenth century. One section of the population of Paris was affected at the centre of the immense Parisian catchment area dominated by anti-clericalism and studded with instances of revolutionary commitment. If we acknowledge the participation of opposing ideologies whose interest was in setting white against black, the Republican tradition on the one hand and counter-revolutionary tradition on the other, we shall understand more exactly why the break was overestimated, with additional assistance from that tradition which seeks to maintain the confrontation between the two camps.

2. Continuity

The revolutionary crisis gave rise to a religious resistance whose effects have been in some cases transient in others lasting. It is no longer possible to accept the traditional explanation without numerous reservations, for it would restrict such resistance to regions with the following characteristics:
—a large majority of insubordinate priests and considerable clandestine practice;
—archaicism and ignorance: Alsace, the Franche-Comté, and the Manche, which were at the head of the list for instruction, resisted de-christianisation. The Nièvre, the Allier, the Cher and the Limoges regions, however, which were at the bottom of the literacy lists, were very open to it.
—pronounced counter-revolutionary beliefs, and royalism, which was the case neither in Flanders, nor in the Moselle, nor at Nice. Resistance for the most part extended over the 'white' territories of the nineteenth century, as Michel Lagrée has shown for l'Île-et-Vilaine, Michael Bée for Normandy, and Louis Pérouas for the Limoges region. the impetus came only from aristocrats or priests.[10] The latter however do not often appear 'for' much at all.

Therefore we have to consider the possibility of a previously dense pastoral activity. But scientific study in this respect is a recent phenomenon and, moreover, incomplete, owing much to the questions asked by Gabriel Le Bras and to the preliminary studies in electoral sociology carried out with André Siegfried. After the example of such work, historians now spontaneously undertake regressive analyses with reference to observed mid-twentieth-century behaviour. Attracted by the recent French school of historians of 'mentalities', they follow Fernand Braudel in looking at long-term developments. They have begun to demonstrate a previously unnoticed continuity between the *ancien régime* and 1850. The same applies to the existence of a religious resurgence around the 1760s, also positively indicated by an increase in the number of illegitimate births or the number of abstentions from Easter duties. There is a strong impression of disaffected upper classes attracted by the optimistic climate characteristic of the last decades of the eighteenth century: an aspiration to happiness, an antithesis of reason and revelation. The deism of the philosophers and their theory of 'useful religion', together with their anti-Christianity, influenced preaching, which would seem to have played down Jesus Christ, 'the great unknown'.[11] This is confirmed by episcopal testimony from 1811: 'Jesus Christ is unknown among us'. Finally, historians are confronted by quite long-lived religious boundaries. The Revolution disclosed them, and often had to be content with widening the gaps in lukewarm and indifferent areas, while fervour was stimulated by persecution elsewhere.

There was a fairly strong lay contribution to the maintenance of rites, when a lack of priests made room for lay initiative. There is the case of the 1,174 signatories of the petition of the 48 Perche communes which, after summer 1792, claimed that they shared their 'fanaticism' with a vast number of people, who were 'all as fanatical as we are about the same things'. They said that they were expressing the wishes of more than 10,000 citizens who had come together 'simply to preserve the Catholic religion'. Michel Bée stresses the daring of a claim which questioned the 'imposture of the atheist representatives of Catholic people' in an area which gave no evidence of a Christian bloc in the nineteenth century.[12]

Often women came forward to maintain or revive worship. It was through religion, and by resisting military conscription, that women were able so spontaneously to take part in political life. Timothy Tackett, for example, has shown this in regard to Sommières in the Gard.[13] The most resolute individuals were bachelors and widows.

The most recent scholarship in this area focuses on aspects of religious defence. In one place the priest might have to be defended. In another it would be worship, which shows clearly that religion and attachment to the clergy do not always go exactly hand in hand. When they were close to the people, the priests succeeded in grouping a strained population round them. This is true where for various reasons the Revolution 'never happened', as Proudhon (from the Comte) and Renan (from Brittany) would say. In such areas continuity for the most part prevailed over breaks, and the restoration of worship preceded the Concordat.

Nevertheless, a fringe section of French people were inclined to protect the popular forms of worship more than ministers, beginning with Sunday Mass and free access to the church. 'White Masses', 'schoolteacher's Masses', or 'lay worship' were features of *departements* outside the counter-revolutionary zones: Aisne, Ardennes, Marne, Normandy, Yonne, Nièvre, Vienne, the western Hérault. Jacques Bernet has shown how keen people were to re-establish public worship in the Compiègne district, where there had been active de-christianisation in the Year II.[14] The hypothesis is tenable that in 1795 a majority of French people favoured public worship, and that renewed continuity prevailed over transitory breaks.

Among the rites to which people had remained most enthusiastically attached, one may cite baptism, the cult of the saints, and attachment to the cross and to church bells. The same is true of the protection of an institution which ensured parish sociability, the confraternities: the Norman *charitons*, the Artois *charitables*, and penitential confraternities of the Pays d'Oc, from the Limoges region to the Nice countryside and Corsica. The law of 18 August 1792 attacking the confraternities was scarcely welcomed. Opinion was mobilised to defend an institution which had a pronounced mutual aid function, another example of the defence of 'real freedoms' (and local freedoms at that), as against the abstract and individualistic liberty of the Rights of Man. There was also a connection between this popular religion and one of the directions of Tridentine Catholicism. Without intending it, the Revolution of the Enlightenment offered Catholicism a strong ally: the popular culture which Ultramontanes around 1850 were inclined to look on less strictly than their rigorist predecessors of the eighteenth century. This alliance is essential to an understanding of the maintenance of loyalty to Catholicism within societies in which the influence of modern economics and social formations was delayed.

The lower-class nature of this religious resistance was observed by the historian Georges Lefebvre in the north. He saw measures directed against the priests who took the oath as a 'great error'.[15] This was also noted by André Latreille, for whom, in his careful synthesis of a history seen from within, the civil Constitution of the Clergy was a grave mistake.[16] Recent ethnographic surveys, like that of 1973 in the Aubrac, in regard to Jean-Pierre Bouissou, 'the Alpuech robber', show an astounding continuity of memory.

Hence, in all aspects of authentic cultural change, continuity must have prevailed over break. Whatever dislike may have been aroused by some of these priests, religion was one of the pillars of popular culture, as were the local dialects which were also persecuted. The local populations showed that they were more attached to their saints, and to their church bells because they defined the rhythms of everyday and of cyclical time. To try to change something like that meant having to face active or passive resistance. Popular religion resisted. We are less sure about the possibility that these instances of continuity indicate an attachment to the core of Christianity. But who could ever lay hand on heart in this respect? It is probably true of a fraction of Catholics. If continuity prevailed, it was because the change was imposed from above, and the intention was to impose it by force. But it is difficult to conceive of the Revolution as a mere parenthesis. The two Frances were clearly contrasted between 1815 and 1880. A patriotic nation on the one hand, and a resistant nation on the other, each with its own population.

By resisting too individualist a notion of the Rights of Man, Catholics stressed family, local and social rights. In this way they endowed with value the sides of the Republican triangle which represented fraternity. As we know, they hesitated for a long time over equality, and the democratic ethos, after the failure of the two first Christian democracies (1848 and at the end of the nineteenth century) made its impact only very slowly. As for liberty, it is certain that it was not, understandably, a charism of minorities, which means of Protestants. Until the twentieth century liberty attracted only a limited number of liberal Catholics, for the most part neither democrats nor socially inclined, the best exceptions being Frédéric Ozanam and Marc Sangnier.

Emile Poulat showed clearly that the matrix for social Catholicism then its extension into Catholic Action was integralism. Though they were concerned about freedoms, more often traditional than modern, French Catholics and the Roman Church largely distrusted liberalism. Certainly there are traces of this attitude as we approach the end of the twentieth century in all those countries with a Latin and Catholic tradition. 'Between the strong and the weak it is liberty which oppresses and the law which emancipates'—to some extent, surely, Lamennais's dictum is still relevant.

Translated by J. G. Cumming

Notes

1. Serge Bianchi, *La Révolution culturelle de l'An II* (Paris 1982).

2. Germain Sicard, 'La Révolution française et l'éducation', in *L'Enfant*, Vol. 39 (1975), pp. 265–295.

3. A paper by Ruth Graham which is to appear in the published proceedings of the Chantilly Colloquium, 'La Vie Religieuse en France et dans les pays occupés a l'époque révolutionnaire' (November 1986).

4. Claude Langlois, *Le catholicisme au féminin* (Paris 1984).

5. *Cf.* n. 3 above.

6. Gerard Cholvy and Yves-Marie Hilaire, *Histoire religieuse de la France contemporaine*, Vol. 1: 1800–1880 (Toulouse 1985), Ch. 99: 'Une géographie religieuse de la France', pp. 259–312.

7. *Cf. Matériaux pour l'Histoire religieuse du peuple français*, Vols. 1 and 2 published (Paris 1982–1986).

8. *Cf.* n. 3 above: Gérard Cholvy, 'Une révolution culturelle? Le test des prénoms'. S. Bianchi relies on 'spontaneity' (see n. 1 above) but the number of first names is unimpressive, and out of a total of 430, 180 are inconclusive (Rose, Marguérite, Colombe, Julienne, Victoire . . .).

9. In 1801 Fr Jauffret issued a call to women: *Des services que les femmes peuvent rendre à la religion* (Paris 1801).

10. See G. Cholvy, 'La Révolution française et la question religieuse', *L'Histoire*, No. 72 (November 1984).

11. F. P. Bowman, *Le Christ romantique* (Geneva, 1973).

12. *Cf.* n. 3 above.

13. *Cf.* n. 3 above.

14. *Recherches de la déchristianisation dans le district de Compiègne* (1789–1795), thesis (Paris 1981).

15. *Les paysans du Nord pendant la Révolution française* (Paris 1924).

16. *L'Eglise catholique et la Révolution française* (1946–, 1950).

Joseph Comblin

The French Revolution: A Bourgeois Revolution

TO THE European bourgeoisie, the French Revolution is the revolution par excellence. For the European bourgeoisie has a universal conscience: in fact, it claims to have the universal conscience. For others—that is the non-bourgeois of the First World and the citizens of the other worlds—the French Revolution was the bourgeois revolution. It furthered the rise of the bourgeoisie in France and in the world, with all the positive and negative consequences of this event.

The French Revolution was not inevitable. It was not impossible for the bourgeoisie to rise to power by other means. It was a combination of circumstances which saw that the bourgeoisie rose to power by means of a revolution. Neither these circumstances, taken in isolation, nor their combination were necessary. One may even say that the bourgeoisie was dragged into a revolution which it had neither foreseen nor wanted. But it was capable of using it as the instrument of its social and political rise, creating irreversible situations.

It is practically certain that if the bourgeoisie had known in advance everything that was going to happen after 1789, it would have done everything possible to avoid the Revolution and would have sided with the conservative aristocracies while waiting for circumstances to improve. In fact, everywhere except in France, this is what the bourgeoisie did, and still does today.

1. The bourgeois character of the French Revolution

The bourgeoisie was the only social class which had a programme of social change and which knew what it wanted. It was the only class to have an achievable programme. It knew how to turn the energies of the popular masses to its own advantage and it emerged from the 25 years of revolutionary crisis as the great victor.

(a) The programme of the bourgeoisie

The programme had already been clearly formulated when Turgot, Louis XVI's minister from 1774 to 1776 tried to put it into effect. The bourgeoisie wanted a more effective exploitation of the land, commercial free enterprise, efficient administration of a unified national territory, the abolition of all privileges which hindered the development of national resources, and a fairer system of taxation.

Such a programme did not necessarily demand a revolution and could even have been introduced by stages. But Turgot failed. On his way, he encountered the rigidity of enlightened despotism and the blindness of an aristocracy which was unable to recognise the signs of the times. A small minority of 400,000 people stood in the way of the progress of a race of 25 millions.

(b) The role of the peasants

The demands of the Third Estate might have led only to a certain reformist unrest ending in the suppression of a few privileges. The king and the aristocracy would have made some concessions. But the meeting of the States General coincided with a disastrous economic situation: two bad harvests had reduced the peasantry to starvation. What turned the demands of the Third Estate into a revolution was the peasant uprising, the Great Fear of late July and early August 1789. Three weeks after the 14 July, the feudal structure of France was in tatters, as was the machinery of monarchy. On 4 August, the aristocrats renounced privileges which in practice no longer existed: there was no longer any way of suppressing the peasant uprising.

The peasant uprisings destroyed established systems but did not create new ones. The bourgeoisie regained control. It created a political system based on representation according to property qualification, which eliminated the political influence of the peasants. And the greater part of the lands which were confiscated from the nobility or the clergy finally ended up in the hands of the bourgeois or of rich farmers who may be compared to them. Doubtless the peasants emerged from the Revolution with some advantages, at least in general terms, because they gained from the suppression of all feudal rights, but those who profited most were the bourgeois, whom the peasants put in the place of the nobles and the clerics.

(c) The role of ideology

The ideology of the French Revolution was formulated from the start, at least in its fundamental points, by the *Declaration of the Rights of Man and the Citizen*, a document in 17 articles, voted by the Constituent Assembly on the 26 August 1789, not without encountering many reservations, especially among the bourgeoisie. The immediate sources of this ideology are to be found in the philosophers of the eighteenth century. They were converted into reality by freemasonry and the other secret societies.

There were very soon discrepancies between the *Declaration* and the various revolutionary Assemblies. These practised what has been called a 'cloaked policy', that is to say that they were wary of putting this *Declaration* into effect. Yet the text of the *Declaration* itself was sufficiently ambiguous and laden with restrictions not to cause too much trouble to the bourgeoisie. It was first and foremost a war machine against the aristocracy. It was not conceived as capable of being invoked against the bourgeoisie, the new dominant class.

Liberty was above all a protection against the arbitrary power of the kings and the nobility. Equality was above all equality before the law. The Revolution recognised the inequalities justified by social convenience. It did not call economic inequalities into question. Property was proclaimed a natural and indefeasible right of man, inviolable and sacred. But this was of no concern to the vast majority of citizens who had no property.

Curiously, the Rights of Man pass as the great innovation of the French Revolution. In reality, the bourgeoisie was able to make a propaganda machine out of this, a rationalisation and a justification of its power. It has continued to do so successfully until the present day. In fact, under an appearance of universality, the rights of man defined a situation which created better conditions for the bourgeoisie, but abandoned the great majority of people without support.

Liberty was defined as being the right to do whatever does no harm to anyone else. Only the bourgeois could turn such a liberty to their advantage.

Equality was above all the rule of law imposed on everyone, but the bourgeois would be able to make laws which favoured themselves. As far as property was concerned, properties were assigned to the bourgeois. In fact, the right to property became abstract and absolute: it was the right to dispose of one's wealth as one pleased. This idea of property suited commercial capitalism and would soon suit industrial and financial capitalism. All the old constraints placed on feudal property by numerous customs or for religious reasons disappeared. The bourgeois could now do whatever he liked with his money.

(d) The role of the Convention, the Jacobins and the Sans-Culottes

Within the French Revolution which was bourgeois, there was another revolution which did not actually come to have a real existence: this was the failed revolution of the Jacobins and the Sans-Culottes, of Robespierre and the Convention. In spite of its wishes, this revolution also served the interests of the bourgeoisie in the end.

Faced with invasion from outside and disorder within, the bourgeois of the Revolution were divided: the moderates wanted to back-pedal. But a left-wing element, the Jacobins, became radical and chose to go forward at speed. To save the Revolution, they insisted that dictatorship was essential. To support them in the streets, they counted on the Sans-Culottes who were not yet an organised proletariat, but a heterogeneous crowd made up of day labourers, craftsmen, small shopkeepers and others, all poor and with the common characteristic of resentment against the rich. They all wanted to defend small holdings, full employment ensured by the State, and the protection of salaries. They were the ancestors of anarchists.

In fact the Jacobin Convention saved the Revolution and France, thanks to dictatorship and thanks to the Terror. It created the revolutionary army to fight against the foreigner and it created repression, two legacies which the bourgeoisie would not be able to rid themselves of later. Once the enemy from outside and from inside had been conquered, the fate of the Convention was fixed. Robespierre could not be a Lenin: he had neither a working class nor a party at his disposal. The moderates triumphed immediately. The modern bourgeoisie received from the hands of the Convention a rescued France and a consolidated Revolution. And from now on, against all the threats from the poor, it would be able to brandish the frightening spectre of the Terror. The cause of the poor would be the Terror. This argument is still in use today.

2. The historical legacy of the French Revoltuion

(a) The bourgeois Nation

The French Revolution finally founded the Nation. It established its complete sovereignty. Nationalism became the dominant ideology, and the Nation the supreme point of reference for all men. The Nation was no longer embodied in concrete realities, but in the State. In the last resort, it was to the State that every citizen owed his loyalty. The Revolution tended to suppress all intermediaries between the individual and the Nation. This isolation was supposed to guarantee the liberty of the individual: the law was supposed to protect him and guarantee his rights. The State, rational, organised, effective, increasingly omnipresent, the State, taking on more and more functions, was the heir to the Revolution. Now, this State was, in fact, bourgeois. It was in the hands of the bourgeois, it established a social structure which promoted the bourgeoisie, it opened the way to bourgeois initiatives and it spread a bourgeois culture.

(b) The poor and the proletariat

The Revolution established a society in which there was no place for the poor. They were supposed not to exist, for their rights were officially guaranteed. Yet the bourgeois revolution would allow industrialisation to create a proletariat of infinite poverty. The bourgeoisie had nothing to offer the proletariat except the crumbs from the feast. Faced with the rise of the proletariat, the bourgeoisie was divided: the majority hardened its position. But a minority became radical and promoted a proletarian revolution.

The memory of the Revolution became ambiguous. For the majority of bourgeois, revolution from now on had to be opposed: the memories of the Terror and the Jacobins would sustain the anguish provoked by working-class and socialist movements. For the others, the radicals, the French Revolution was to be begun again or prolonged. A second phase of it was missing. For some the Revolution was the past, not to be interfered with: for others it was the future. The memory of the Revolution gave rise to revolutionary parties, first of the masses, then of professionals. The socialist revolutions claimed to be the continuation of the French Revolution, but for the moderate bourgeois they were the exact opposite. As is well-known, the European proletariat was divided. One half was taken over by the bourgeoisie in return for the concessions of social-democracy. The other half provided today's communist world with its troops.

A basic ambiguity has remained. Even in Europe, the French Revolution was not everyone's revolution and it did not affect everyone in the same way.

(c) War

War played a major role in the Revolution. it consolidated it by binding the Nation together, providing a great system of symbols and a culture. The army was the place where the revolutionary Nation was forged. The war was the Nation at arms. The mass rising of citizens laid the foundations for what would later become total war and the doctrine of National Security.

In principle, the bourgeoisie is democratic. But every time that democracy might turn against it, it appeals to the army, or to a military regime. The appeal to Bonaparte constituted a precedent which still serves today. The bourgeoisie is never completely democratic. It thinks it can make use of the army with impunity, but often it is the army which is making use of it.

The French Revolution proclaimed peace to the world, in theory. But it also claimed for itself the mission of coming to the help of peoples who wanted to conquer tyranny. But who would be the judge? When all is said and done it would be the national interest. The Revolution founded an interventionist and even an imperial tradition. Was it by chance that in the nineteenth century bourgeois Europe succeeded for the first time in creating a practically universal Empire? The legacy of the Revolution also included the mission to 'liberate' all peoples, economically, of course, but also by force of arms when the economic measures met with resistance. European expansionism had no need of the French Revolution in order to assert itself. But it did not find any real restraints in it. On the contrary, it found additional motivation.

(d) The Revolution and the colonies

Santo Domingo (which became Haiti) was the finest jewel of the French colonial Empire of this period. With the announcement of the events of 1789, the white planters of the colony tried to do what the colonisers of Spanish America did a generation later: proclaim their allegiance to the King, but assert a certain independence. The Revolutionary Assemblies never considered independence; but the Constituent Assembly proclaimed the rights of citizens, not only the whites, but also mulattos and liberated blacks. Neither the Constituent nor the Legislative Assembly, however, proclaimed the liberation of slaves. Faced with disagreements between the white powers, the slaves revolted and succeeded in expelling their representatives. In the hope of recovering the colony, the Convention declared the freedom of slaves, but it was too late. After Thermidor the abolition of slavery was revoked. Napoleon attempted to reconquer the colony and sent an army in 1803. The army finally broke down the military resistance of the blacks, but succumbed to yellow fever, and within a few weeks 15,000 soldiers died of the disease. The remains of the army took refuge in various ports and had to surrender to the English.

Haiti was the first independent republic south of the United States. It served as an example for the whole of Latin America, or rather it served as a deterrent. For the elite of the Spanish and Portuguese empires more important than independence was the necessity to avoid a repetition of the events in Haiti. They needed an independence without the freedom of slaves, or even of the Indians.

Slavery had been abolished in France after 1761 but it was not part of the Revolutionary programme to extend this abolition to the colonies or to grant these colonies their independence.

3. The peripheral influence of the French Revolution

The French Revolution was not responsible for the conduct of the followers which it inspired in all the nations of the world, and particularly in the Third World. However, there was a certain continuity between master and followers. In the development of the ideals of the French Revolution throughout the world, there was certainly already a seed in the Revolution itself, especially in its bourgeois character. We will mention here only the case of Latin America, which seems a good example.

To an equal, and probably greater extent than the American Revolution, the French Revolution was welcomed enthusiastically by a majority of the literate public in the Spanish and Portuguese colonies. The ideas of the Revolution stimulated certain spokesmen of the independence movements. And yet, nowhere was there an equivalent of the French Revolution. The movements and the wars of independence installed new conservative states everywhere. The ideology of the Revolution served from time to time, but there was no bourgeoisie to give a practical direction to this ideology. There was no connection between the society of the new nations and contemporary French society.

(a) The separation of ideology and practice

During the last two centuries, after the failure of independence, the Latin-American elite assimilated the ideology of the French Revolution with a faultless spirit of imitation: the rights of man, democracy, liberalism. This ideology became part of constitutions, laws and official pronouncements. It formed the common language of the ruling classes. But practice is another matter. It was still the old aristocracies that governed, with the help of the armed forces whenever necessary. Revolutionary speech masked a conservative reality. This was because there was no bourgeoisie, and, lacking a bourgeoisie, the Latin-American nations could not carry out any bourgeois revolution.

Over the decades, traces of a bourgeoisie have certainly emerged: a kind of commercial, industrial or service bourgeoisie, a semblance of an intellectual class at the service of this semblance of a bourgeoisie. As one of the authorities on Latin-American sociology, Leopoldo Zea, has said: 'One of the problems for our sociologists is the definition of this middle class which aspires to become a bourgeoisie. Is it a pseudo-bourgeoisie? Is it a rural bourgeoisie? Is it a bourgeoisie which is based on the export of raw materials?'[1]

The Latin-American bourgeoisie is merely the extension of a metropolitan bourgeoisie formerly situated in England, France, Germany and today especially in the United States and Japan. Such a pseudo-bourgeoisie has not the power to create even a bourgeois revolution. For the metropolitan powers rely on the old corrupt aristocracies who support them. They strengthen the armed forces when necessary to guarantee the continuity of the past. As for what an independent bourgeoisie might be, it is in too much of a minority to play a decisive role in society. For a long time, leftists have been looking for the 'national bourgeoisie' which has been shown to be a mere phantom.

A French Revolution cannot be carried out only with ideas and convictions. A bourgeoisie is needed. This was lacking in Latin-America, hence there was no French Revolution there.

(b) The legal state: reality and fiction

The French Revolution created the legal State. All the nations of the world have adopted the model. But behind the model there is most frequently nothing but a void. The legal State is a fiction.

During the course of this decade of the '80s, most of the Latin-American nations have moved from an openly military regime to an officially democratic regime following western forms, but the change is only illusory. Behind the appearance of a civil government, it is still the military who rule. Officially, there is a separation of the powers, but in reality, neither the legislative nor the judiciary enjoys a true independence. Officially it is the law which rules, but the law only rules the poor, for the rich are exempted whenever necessary. As the proverb says: 'A rich man has never been seen in prison.' Officially, taxes are divided among the citizens, but a rich man has never been seen to pay taxes. Officially, education is compulsory, but a third of children have no school to go to and in Brazil there are 8 million abandoned children roaming the streets.

'Official language is mad, and its lunacy is the normality of the system. "There will be no devaluation", say the Ministers of Finance on the day before the currency crash. "Agricultural reform is our main objective", say the Ministers of Agriculture while extending the latifundia. "There is no censorship", say the Ministers of Culture in the countries where the vast majority of people cannot have books because of the price or illiteracy.'[2]

Countries such as Uruguay and Argentina have promulgated laws absolving crimes of torture, while these same countries have ratified the international convention against torture which condemns any such absolution. And so on, and so on. The legal State is a fiction. It only applies in so far as it suits the interests of the small minority of less than one per cent of the population which has inherited authority from the colonial powers.

(c) What revolution?

If a revolution equivalent to the French Revolution is impossible in Latin America for lack of a bourgeoisie, what sort of revolution can there be then?

For a long time, revolutionaries have defended the classic thesis that before any proletarian revolution there must be a bourgeois revolution. But the bourgeoisie is missing. Can a proletarian revolution take place before a bourgeois revolution? It was tried in Chile, but it failed. Is a revolution, based on the alliance of the peasant class and an avant-garde of professional revolutionaries, as happened in Cuba and Nicaragua, possible elsewhere? The first requirement for this is a large peasant class. This class is rapidly disappearing in Latin America. And then, you need the collapse of the established State. Can a hardened revolutionary party bring about the collapse of the State? The 'Sendero luminoso' in Peru firmly believes so. How many years will be needed to achieve this result?

Who can a revolution count on? Certainly not on the metropolitan powers. These are the faithful allies of the established order and the traditional dominant classes. The support which the First World countries claim to give to democratisation movements is also a mere fiction. The First World countries want a democratic fiction. That is why their representatives travel all over the world with what Eduardo Galeano calls a 'democracy meter':[3] they measure everywhere the amount of separation of power, of so-called free elections, of so-called democratic laws, in short the amount of outward appearance of democracy, and award each country a diploma of democracy with a mark corresponding to its merits. All that is a game of fiction. For the bourgeoisies which rule the western nations today have no interest in the democratisation of the Third World. Their interest is in the status quo, even if for that they have to support the worst criminals, as they still do today in Chile, Paraguay and Central America. The legal State is not an item of export except at the cultural level for propaganda.

This is why even a bourgeois revolution is possible only after a profound Western crisis, and a collapse of its unity or its political, military and economic strength. Social systems fall or change more through the collapse of what supported them than by the strength of those who promote change. The ruling elites in Latin America only survive through the support given them by western bourgeoisies. They will fall together.

The peasant class is disappearing, the working class is declining because of automation. What is the value and the future of the vast urban sub-proletariat of the present great megalopolises (Mexico, 19 millions, Sao Paulo, 15 millions)? What are determined revolutionary parties like the 'Sondero luminoso' of Peru capable of achieving? In this uncertainty, what is the future of projects for democratisation, or the rights of man? Fiction and more fiction? Will the people have their say one day? At the time of writing, Brazil is in the middle of a sociodrama, living through the fiction of a Constituent Assembly which is writing a fiction of a Constitution of a fictional democracy, dictated by generals who are not a fiction, and who are the allies of a class of great landowners, each one the master of tens of thousands of acres, who have just equipped their private militias with the most modern weapons under the complaisant eye of the armed forces. Fiction faced by a very present reality.

This is what the French Revolution has become in the world, this is its historical heritage. Is it completely without blame? In history how do we apportion innocence or guilt?

Translated by Barrie Mackay

Notes

1. Leopoldo Zea, *Latinoamerica: Emancipación y neocolonialismo* (ed. Tiempo Nuevo, Caracas 1971), p. 156.

2. *Cf.* Eduardo Galeano, 'América latina: La democracia aparente', in the review *Solidaridad*, (Bogotá, Year 10, No. 91, 1988), p. 32.

3. *Cf.* Eduardo Galeano, *op. cit.*, p. 39.

Jean Moussé

Catholic Thought and Liberalism: Discussion Arising from a Book

HAS CATHOLIC theology thought about liberalism? For Michael Novak, the author of a recently translated American work, the answer is no.[1] Catholicism lags behind in the dream of a socialism inspired by faith. It has never really thought about the evangelical dimensions of a 'democratic capitalism', of which the United States presents the model. The criticism is harsh. But understanding its significance and drawing lessons from it are more important than lagging behind.

Jean-Yves Calvez, in his preface to the French edition, emphasises an originality for which another author is actually responsible.[2] He places it 'in the theory of the three distinct sectors (not completely separated but not completely merged): political, economic, ethico-cultural. The ethico-cultural being the sphere of religious knowledge, of universities and cultural associations of every sort. As you say, real freedom is necessary for each of these sectors in relation to the two others'.[3] That, indeed, is the question.

I

This theory of the three sectors expressed the fragmentation of modern times. Conceptually it is in keeping with the philosophy of the Enlightenment, politically with the fundamental principles of American democracy and the French Revolution, and economically with the creation of a world-wide market. That is the challenge which Catholic theology should be able to take up. Max Weber has described the events which seem to have led to this modern fragmentation. Over the centuries, the expansion

71

of towns, the formation of the bourgeois class, and the networks of international trade had undermined the foundations of aristocratic and rural society. At the start of the industrial age, Adam Smith noticed the fragmentation of the economic society open to the world market. Within an interactive network of complementary activities, no one authority can any longer dominate movements which, in the course of time, will be made more and more unpredictable by the acceleration of change. Modern society (Gesellschaft) supplants the community (Gemeinschaft) which formerly characterised Christendom.

We are today at the heart of this upheaval which redistributes the three political, economic and ethico-cultural powers. No political force can lay claim to world hegemony, and any force seeking to reach that point could only do so at the cost of intolerable violence. According to the rules of the planetary game, the economy is made up of interdependences which no single part of the system can dominate. Christianity itself no longer claims to be the only way to salvation. The Revelation, whose message it carries, has been offered, according to Karl Rahner and many others, to all men from the beginning. In such a society, the *contract*, guaranteed politically by the right to property and morally by the respect for the 'rights of man', has supplanted traditions regarded as sacred. Money, by the possibilities which it offers and the constraints which it imposes has become the main instrument of control in society.

Each of the three sectors is autonomous, but each also needs the other two. The economy avoids political voluntarism and moral constraints, but it calls for political control and if there was no ethics it would lose all human direction. Politics controls movements which it cannot dominate, but it is the economy which feeds the citizens and ethics which gives them direction. Ethics, which gives its message to religions, would not exist if it did not take form in politico-economic reality.

II

In evoking the theory of the three sectors, Jean-Yves Calvez emphasises that they are 'neither completely separate, nor completely merged'. The whole question is to know exactly how they are linked. The answer can only confirm the views of Novak at the same time challenging Catholic thought.

If the three sectors of politics, economics and ethico-culture do not overlap, they at least have a common origin in the existence of individuals who must participate in all three in order to live. The freedom of men is thus the only area where the three dimensions, political, economic, and religious or ethic can come together in harmony. Novak finds there a justification of liberal arguments.

Christianity has nothing to lose by opening itself up to these views. Was not the Gospel which it proclaims the bearer of a message of radical liberation? In the name of truth, freedom and the love that bound Him to His Father, did Jesus not call in question the legalist system instituted by His people, the rigidity of which He changed drastically, along with their messianic illusions and racial pretensions. How would these values not match those of the market economy: 'from the encouragement to self-discipline, work, the spirit of risk, sacrifices agreed for a better future, to the insistence on generosity, integrity, social change and care for the common good'?

But it is understood, as the introduction to the work emphasises, that the question is not the same in the United States as it is in Europe. The United States were founded by immigrants who were freed from the cultural constraints of the societies they were escaping from, and forced to accept themselves as different. They had no 'order' to defend and everything to invent. Their religious communities worked by themselves, without pretensions to hegemony, as forces among so many others. It is quite another matter for the churches in Europe, caught up in the memory of a weighty past. They remember the time, now past, when the religious and political authorities, referring to the same Gospel, argued over whether Prince or Pope should have the upper hand. And it is there, according to Novak, that the answer to our question should be sought: Catholicism has never thought about liberalism because it lingers over the memory of Christianity.

III

Since the beginning, the Church, through the liberty of its members inspired by faith, has been working for freedom, peace, truth and justice. It is the essence of its mission. But to fulfil it, it had to organise itself into a community, carrying a tradition, capable of solemnising rites, encouraging mutual aid among its members. The first of these two aspects has lost nothing today, but the same cannot be said of the second. In fact, the Catholic Church has organised itself according to a cultural model inspired by the concept of community (Gemeinschaft) which it has claimed to prolong, while the modern world, in its fragmentation, was changing into society (Gesellschaft). It has resisted change in the name of a tradition which it had no reason to regard as sacred but which rather served as a pretext for the maintenance of a certain series of powers. On this point, Novak's criticism is perfectly explicit: 'It is particularly difficult for religious bodies to slip into a role which takes all authority from them and places them outside the centre of things. Their natural inclination is to imbue every dimension of life with their own vision, with what gives a divine sense to human nature and its destiny. Humans being social animals, creatures of flesh and blood, the religious authorities in their heart of hearts think that they should rightly resist this shelving of their power. They aspire to a public social role. In democratic capitalism, this role is not refused them, but it is neither a central position nor one of authority'.[4]

Here it can be understood how Paul VI's criticism of liberalism, quoted by Jean-Yves Calvez in his preface can seem ambiguous. This system, according to the sovereign pontiff, 'considers social realities as more or less automatic consequences of individual initiatives, and not as an aim of social organisation and one of the essential criteria by which the quality of this organisation may be appreciated'.[5] But what exactly is implied in this criticism?

We might think that the Pope is attacking the degrading nature of anthropocentrism and the domineering and possessive will which feed the violence of selfishness in liberal society. The permanence of poverty and the scandal of glaring inequalities could in fact justify his position and he must certainly have thought about it when publishing a text which, in other respects, approves of the struggle for freedom in the face of the claims of political powers. But does the community ideal which the criticism underlies accede to the fragmentation of modern society or not? And if it does, how is it to be expressed in the organisation and administration of an ecclesiastical community which must from now on abandon any dream of a return to a Christian world. How can free 'individuals', responsible for their actions before God and before men in every area of their political, economic and religious activity relate differently to the institutions whose dealings are clearly stated in their freedom? How can they be organised in a Church to live and bear witness to the Gospel in this fragmented world? How can an authority which is exercised first and foremost in the direction of freedom and service for all men function if it abandons all claim to hegemony in any possible area?

The question raised by Michael Novak is to know how the movement of charity which inspires the life of the Church can be served by an authority which breaks courageously with its medieval traditions by acceding to a liberating movement which is close to the gospel spirit and, what is more, conforms to the spirit which inspires the world today.

The question is formidable, and we cannot be surprised at the remarks of a prelate denouncing 'the spirit of enlightenment'. He is right to discover there the main challenge offered to the Church of today. But the danger is not where he situates it. It will not be removed by a return to a Christian world, a temptation which rises to the surface everywhere. Christendom is dead. The Church can only live in the acknowledgment, transfigured by faith, of a spirit of freedom alone capable of giving direction to renewed institutions including the Church.

The question, of course, goes far beyond the limits of these few pages. But that was no reason for not raising it.

Translated by Barrie Mackay

Notes

1. M. Novak, *Une éthique économique (les valeurs de l'économie de marché)* (Paris 1987); (*The Spirit of Democratic Capitalism* 1982).

2. D. Bell, *Les contradictions du capitalisme* (Paris 1979); (*The Cultural Contradictions of Capitalism*, New York 1976).

3. *Loc. cit.* p. VII.

4. *Ibid.* p. 76.

5. *Ibid.* p. IX.

Daniele Menozzi

The Significance of the Catholic Reaction to the Revolution

1. The antithesis of Catholicism and revolution

'A LOATHING of any religious and social order not established by human beings and which they did not control completely; the proclamation of human rights wholly contrary to divine intentions; the foundation of a new religious and social order created by human beings and ruled independently of divine will; in short, the apotheosis of humankind which, as has been shown, is the very essence of revolution: revolution as it really is, and revolution as it now threatens Europe and finds in destruction its true fulfilment.'[1]

Those were the terms in which, shortly after the midpoint of the nineteenth century, the Abbé Gaume, one of the most important representatives of intransigent and Ultramontane Catholic culture, described the results of his researches into the evils afflicting contemporary society. In his opinion the French Revolution was, so to speak, the litmus paper disclosing a long-term process affecting humanity: an attempt to secularise human society completely, to deprive the Church of its direction of society, and to exclude all forms of Catholic influence on the forms and ways of human association. Consequently, Gaume summarised a judgment which had gradually permeated the Catholic world since the events of 1789. By the time his book was published (1856), its message was for the most part synonymous with Catholic public opinion insofar as it was interested in social questions. It was to remain the common legacy of Catholic culture until the second Vatican Council. It even survived the Council in more restricted anti-conciliar and traditionalist circles.[2]

Nevertheless, it is true to say that nineteenth-century liberal Catholicism arrived at a different judgment—in regard, at least, to the ideas expressed by pundits of the Constituent Church under the French Revolution. For example, one interesting supporter of such a viewpoint was Canon G. Audisio, who was able to write, even in 1876, that the legacy of 1789 was not to be rejected in its entirety, inasmuch as liberty, equality and fraternity 'are certainly reconsecrated as principles of nature and of the Gospel', and therefore the requisite 'social restoration' of the contemporary world should take as its starting-point those values 'which Jesus Christ bequeathed to us'.[3] Apart from the fact that his book was put on the Index, and forgetting that liberal Catholicism was repeatedly condemned by the popes, it is clear that such circles were still fundamentally convinced that the concepts of socio-political organisation that arose with the Revolution were acceptable; that is, they were acceptable insofar as they were reconcilable with the fundamentals of religion and, thus relegitimated, could even become an integral part of the teaching of the Church. After all, the tendencies of liberal Catholicism betray the considerable extent to which they were actually subordinate to the central tenets of Ultramontanism, according to which there could be no truly human and civil form of social organisation which was not based on religion.

Gaume's judgments, therefore, though not uniformly shared, were conducive to an actual hegemony in Catholicism. They comprised a compact and consistent theory: the French Revolution was the last link in a process which began with the Renaissance and the Protestant Reformation, continued through the Englightenment, and showed its true face quite unmistakably with the Terror and de-christianisation. Even when those events were over, the spirit which had revealed its character in the Revolution—the desire to destroy all forms of social presence of the Church—continued to plague Europe and the world in an ongoing collision (which had now reached a radical and definitive stage) between the only two forces which could contend for control of the earthly city: Catholicism and, of course, revolution. This view of things gave rise to the ultimate thesis of Ultramontanism: the necessity for the faithful to ensure a favourable outcome to the conflict. To do this they would have to tackle society directly and revive the directive function of the Church in regard to human society, and in particular restore to the papacy its supreme function of control over social life—the function, indeed, which it had exercised in the Middle Ages and which the Renaissance and the Reformation, with their exaltation of individual rights, had first put into a state of crisis.

This is not an appropriate place to examine the elements and various versions of this comprehensive interpretation of modern history and of the accordant myth of a return to medieval Christianity.[4] It is pertinent instead to show how this imaginary prospect—which in the long run strongly conditioned the attitude of Catholics to society—arose in connection with the revolutionary events and was then espoused by the papal magisterium.

2. Origins of an interpretation

On 10 March 1791 Pius VI issued the brief *Quod aliquantum* in which he condemned the Civil Constitution of the Clergy, and the comprehensive re-organisation of the French Church which the Constituent Assembly had approved the year before. They had adjusted the diocesan administrative districts to the new departmental administrative divisions; attributed to the metropolitans of the new institution canonical faculties in respect of new bishops which were traditionally reserved to the pope; and put the electoral college in charge of the nomination of ecclesiastics charged with the cure of souls (parish priests and bishops). The pope did not restrict himself to denouncing this undue invasion of the spiritual sphere by a political entity; he also stated that it was the necessary consequence of the proclamation of the rights of liberty and equality: senseless and irrational in natural terms, those rights were, moreover, quite contrary to divine law, and therefore tended inevitably to violate the Catholic religion.[5] Pius VI nevertheless said that he did not intend to intervene in temporal affairs which were internal to a country, and that he would not declare that the *ancien régime* ought to be re-established. His sole aim was to 'preserve from all attacks the rights of the Church and of the Apostolic See'. This gave the impression that the condemnation of the principles of 1789 was a response to essentially political demands: a matter of asserting that an eventual recognition would be tied to a re-examination by revolutionary France of the Civil Constitution of the Clergy.

Two years later, however, the pope addressed a consistory with an allocution commemorating the death of Louis XVI. By now he had wholly abandoned his previous possibilism in favour of an unequivocal rejection of revolutionary principles.[6]

The pope now closely associated absolute monarchy with Catholicism. In his opinion, freedom and equality led inevitably to barbarism and anarchy, thus undermining the sole authentic foundation of collective life, the Catholic religion. It was not so much the obvious emotion felt at the execution of the king which explained this obstinacy, as rather the fact that Pius VI now placed the phenomenon of revolution in a larger and more comprehensive setting: the French events were the result of a conspiracy planned by the supporters of the Reformation, in particular the Calvinists, who to accomplish their designs had entered into an alliance with 'perverse philosophies'. This 'ungodly party', out of hatred of the Church, proposed to 'ruin the Catholic religion' in France and in Europe, and to bring down monarchs and empires which supported it. Thus the French Revolution was taken out of the framework of any political and historical events which were susceptible of rational identification and examination. The only terms which could be used to interpret it now were of the quality of 'plot', 'conspiracy', and 'cabal', and the typical descriptive concept which now became compulsory in papal circles was that of an epoch-making conflict with the Church.

What were the basic reasons for this change in papal thinking? First a number of inescapable facts had to be accommodated somehow: above all the flight of the refractory bishops and their replacement by the Constituent clergy. Then there were the decrees which gradually—as the era progressed unfavourably—became more unyielding and tended to persecution when faced with clergy who had not sworn the oaths of loyalty to the revolutionary regime. There was also the consequent emigration of many clergy to deal with. Finally the papacy had to do something about the September massacres and, in connection with the rebellion in the Vendée, the established equation of Catholic with possible traitor which facilitated the summary execution of priests and faithful. These dramatic occurrences were followed by the traumatic event of de-christianisation (together with the closing of the churches, the use of liturgical vestments for satire and profane celebrations, the forced resignation and marriage of priests) and the simultaneous replacement of Christian worship by new revolutionary cults. Obviously all these events together first provoked then consolidated a highly negative assessment of the Revolution. Moreover the adoption of the Republican calendar, and the removal of Sunday, seemed to evince a desire to organise the division of time in contradistinction to a thousand years of Christian tradition. Nevertheless, reaction to the papal document of 1793 went beyond the mere ascertainment of an irremediable antithesis. To understand the situation properly one must also take into account other ideas and judgments expressed in the Catholic world of the period.

In the final decades of the eighteenth century there were various instances of reflection on contemporary history which were taken up later and reworked into a more organic system. The jurisdictional politics of absolute monarchy, the looming ecclesiastical reform of Josephinism, the suppression of the Jesuits—formalised by Clement XIV—and the growing success of the philosophy of the Enlightenment, with its defence of religious liberty, had induced various ecclesiastical circles to take serious account of the notion of a modern world apparently opposed to ecclesiastical guidance.[7] Some commentators thought that in this conflict it was possible for the papacy to employ against the disobedient agents of political power the same temporal instruments—such as excommunication and interdicts—which had ensured the success of the medieval theocracy. Others dwelled on pessimistic forecasts: inevitably divine anger would be visited on modern society, with frightful results. Yet others began to advance various theories about the meaning of present events. The ex-Jesuit Diessbach, for example, maintained that the contemporary crisis of the Church could be understood only in terms of a satanic plot operating in history. Beginning with Luther's rebellion—which tended to replace the authority of the Church with the authority of the individual—that satanic plan was now being realised through libertine atheism and enlightenment philosophy, which were movements that intended to destroy the control of the Church over civil society.

The perceived characteristics of the Revolution and the progressive exacerbation of the conflict with Catholicism made sure that these various elements were eventually combined in one neat and consistent set of ideas and images. An initial trace is to be found in the writings in which the Catholic opponents of the changed regime, above all of the Civil Constitution of the Clergy, set down their reactions to such events. A theory was adumbrated according to which the Revolution was a punishment which Providence had visited on human beings, and in particular on the Church, in order to show divine disapproval of the Church's inadequate resistance to the impious nature of the modern world.[8] The emergence of two equally important aspects must be stressed: on the one hand, divine anger was visited on a Church which had not adequately opposed politico-social change in the name of maintenance of tradition; on the other hand, revolutionary elan was designed to have an overall effect on a society which, rather than preserve its attitude of obedient submission to ecclesiastical control of the organisation of collective life, wished to affirm its own autonomy.

These two key notions go very well with the belief that there was some kind of plot behind the revolutionary process: in order to pursue his providential purposes, God had consented to the success of the conspiracy against the throne and the altar hatched by freemasonry, in conjunction with the Jansenists and the 'philosophers'. What is most striking—in spite of the many variants of conspiracy theory spread for the most part by Barruel—is the firm conviction that freemasonry was a direct product of the Protestant Reformation. Thus, for example, J. B. Lefranc, one of the first Catholic opponents of the Revolution, maintained that masonic society was the 'quintessence' of Protestant heresy and that all the seditions of modern history, together with those of the eighteenth century,[9] were to be attributed to it. In this way an image of the Revolution was propagated as the ultimate result of a long chain of errors started by the Lutheran removal of the individual from the power of Rome.

Fed by this intellectual fodder, in 1793 Pius VI adumbrated his version of this antithesis between Catholicism and Revolution. Quite apart from the absolute improbability on an historical level of the suggested theory—which was without any adequate documentary support—an extremely significant tendency in interpretation now made its appearance: the evils of the modern world were henceforth presented as the fruits of a refusal to accept the authority of the Church. In this perspective the sole responsibility of the hierarchy consisted in summoning people to submit to them all their decisions in the politico-social field. The historical process of mankind could interrogate the Church only in one respect: it was duty-bound in fact to indicate more opportune social measures but also to record the fact that misfortune was the fruit of disobedience. In subsequent years a very precise theory in respect of all the foregoing was to emerge.

3. The return to the Middle Ages

All moderate authors, as for example Mallet-Du Pan, quite soon introduced a parallel between the revolutionary events and the Middle Ages: the popular masses in revolt in the contemporary era were 're-enacting' the same onslaught on civilisation which, in the Middle Ages, was waged by the forces of barbarism. The sole difference consisted in the fact that now the aggression had been taken right inside civilisation itself, and was no longer confined to the territories outside.[10] This interpretation was very soon taken up in Catholic circles, which stressed the fact that the Church—and above all the papacy—had to begin to play in the contemporary crisis the same directive and civilising role that it enjoyed in medieval times. The notion of the Church dismissing the errors of the modern world which had followed from the Reformation could be combined very neatly with the idea of overcoming modern errors by returning to the Middle Ages.

An immediate application of this viewpoint appeared in the attempt of a number of Catholic thinkers to persuade the pope to declare—as in the Middle Ages with regard to the crusades—a holy war against the bearers of a satanic revolution which, a veritable daughter of Luther, was destroying religion and civilisation. At the very same time the curia was dreaming of the papal proclamation of a crusade against revolutionary France, in accordance with the express wishes of some members of the

Spanish episcopate. A somewhat more wary line ultimately prevailed: it was restricted to supporting and blessing the action of the counter-revolutionary forces.[11] But the absence of a military approach to the problem did not prevent the elaboration of the idea of a reconstructed medieval Christianity as the sole adequate Catholic response to the historical tendency manifested in 1789.

The De Maistre of *Considérations sur la France* (1796)—not in fact inimical to the desire for an armed struggle—gave the counter-revolution the task of restoring the medieval theocracy, displaced by the Protestantism which had more directly produced Jacobinism. But it was mainly the Vicomte de Bonald, in his *Théorie du Pouvoir politique et religieux* (1793), who put forward a notion which was to enjoy considerable resonance in the Catholic world.[12] In his opinion the medieval papacy, which exercised a supreme political function, had pretended to reunite the peoples of Europe, divided by the barbaric invasions, as a common family, held together by the profession of the same religion. The Reformation produced a rift in that seamless body, and one which had continued to grow from the moment when the various revolutionary movements had burst forth and, in the course of three centuries, had put into disarray that same European civil society which was now threatened by complete anarchy. In effect, the disintegrative elements introduced by Luther and Calvin continued to cause trouble. They could be blocked only by reconstructing the hierarchical and sacral society realised in the medieval *respublica christiana*. With such a reconstruction of civilisation, and with the renewal of papal control over human association, in its technocratic form, an indissoluble bond would unite the members of the one family.

This notion met with a success which transcended the confines of the Catholic Church. One of the many testimonies to this fact is *Die Christenheit oder Europa*, written by the German poet Novalis in 1799.[13] Temporarily rejected by a culture which was still suffused with the Enlightenment—so much so that it would see the light only several years later—this document had a profound influence on the disciples of the new romantic ideas. It expressed a profound nostalgia for all aspects of a medieval life guided throughout by religious feeling and controlled by the supreme head of the Church which opposed 'dangerous discoveries in the field of knowledge', and wisely restricted the freedom which could have damaged the prevailing sacral mentality. Into this situation Luther had introduced an element which was destined to destroy permanently the unity of joyous medieval Christianity. The primacy of the Bible and of its interpretation by the individual meant in reality affirming the legitimacy of a continuous revolution. Therefore only the restoration of a uniform

Christianity in which, as in the Middle Ages, the entire political establishment would submit to the power of the papacy, would secure the return of peace and of social stability.

Certainly in Novalis' perspective an upsurge of the spirit rather than the action of the Church would help to bring back a world organised on the basis of Christian values. But his ideas were extremely influential in Protestant circles which retained a preoccupation with political and social changes indebted to the Revolution; thus the 'converts' movement, where the convictions expressed by the Catholic supporters of theocracy matured rapidly.[14] Distaste for the consequences of the Revolution—as is shown clearly by C. L. de Haller—was conducive to making Protestantism fundamentally responsible for the devastation of the existing social order in Europe. Hence the spate of contemporary conversions to Catholicism in the hope that the re-establishment of the papal monarchy would contribute to a society constituted organically and hierarchically. On the other hand, the same currents in the Church of Rome fortified in traditionalist circles the conviction that there existed only two forces which contended with one another for control of history as it developed: the theocratic ideology of Catholicism and the barbaric anarchy of revolution.

It is impossible here to follow the ample debate which ensued on these theses. It is sufficient to remember that in the Catholic world of the Napoleonic age—as was shown in works published in 1802 by the National Institute on 'the influence of the Reformation on the progress of Enlightenment'—there was evidence of that way of articulating judgments and assessments typified by the kind of genealogy that would connect Luther's revolt with the French Revolution.

Nevertheless, with the Restoration these voices became altogether more numerous and insistent as they pointed to medieval Christianity as the paradigmatic model for present use, in an attempt to go beyond a mere reconstruction of the alliance between the throne and the altar. That alliance had been shown to be incapable of resolving the problem which was revealed by the events of 1789 and their consequences.[15] Of course, in the same period the papal magisterium itself adopted the viewpoint which had originated in traditionalist circles and was now proposed to all the faithful.

4. The intervention of the magisterium

In the first place it should be remembered that the papacy adopted not only the intransigent viewpoint but the concomitant appropriation of a whole sector of church life—the formulation of the faith and the condemnation of errors committed by the faithful—which was traditionally relegated to the freedom of theological discussion. This made the directives of the pontifical magisterium all the more binding.[16] Even in 1814 Pius VII asked Louis XVIII not to subscribe to the Constitution, which proclaimed religious freedom and the freedom of the press, and thus not only adversely affected the Church but favoured the rise of sedition and disorder. The pope considered his intervention reasonable inasmuch as he had received from Christ 'the task of ruling Christian society'. This directive power in the civil sector was also cited by his successor, Leo XII, who did not restrict himself to urging in the encyclicals *Ubi primum* (1824) and *Quo graviora* (1824) that Christian princes should translate Christian principles into compulsory norms condemning errors arising from the French Revolution, but in a letter to Louis XVIII directly requested the king to take measures to ensure that France—where contemporary evils had begun—would make itself the bearer of a new model of universal civilisation, in which the definition of temporal questions would be referred to the pope and to the hierarchy.[17]

With *Mirari vos* (1832) of Gregory XVI, the thesis that the Catholic religion constituted the only 'brake' which could obviate the destruction of the political and social order did not refer only to the papal condemnation of modern liberty, but was also associated with the statement that the roots of subversion were to be found in heresy. Indeed, some medieval heretics had aimed at disaffecting constitutive powers, and Luther's rebellion was the origin of the machinations and conspiracies which had plagued the contemporary era.[18] It was above all Pius IX, however, who showed that the viewpoint elaborated by the Catholic reaction to the French Revolution had now been definitively inherited by the magisterium. The pope, who in his programmatic encyclical, *Qui pluribus* (1846), had contrasted Christian civilization, basically the creation of the Church of Rome, with the contemporary disorders which had their major source in the biblical society inherited from Luther, returned to his theme in greater detail in *Nostis et nobiscum*. This was published in 1849 during his exile at Portici, and was therefore affected by his reaction to the Roman Republic.[19]

In this document the pope confirmed the viewpoint that Protestantism, by profaning ecclesiastical provisions, had opened the way to various kinds of insubordination, until eventually that opportune moment was reached when socialism and communism seized the banner of revolutionary subversion. Pius IX answered all difficult questions by reference to the civilising role which the papacy had played with the collapse of the Roman Empire and the barbarian invasions. In this way he may be said to have updated the genealogy of modern errors—for it was now claimed that a direct line ran from the Reformation to communism. Pius IX also said that the sole remedy for the disorder in society must be the recovery of a Christian civilisation: of, that is, an essentially hierocratic order.

This comprehensive view, which started, as we have seen, with the Catholic reaction to the French Revolution, was now associated with Catholic culture and its relations to the contemporary world, and was expressed and adjusted as specific occasions demanded.[20] In fact it was proposed in the Vatican I constitutions *Dei filius* and *Pastor aeternus* (1870) that over against atheism, the product of the Reformation and the mortal enemy of social life, there stood its implacable opponent the papacy, which was the basis of any authoritative means of maintaining a cohesive community.[21] Accordingly, an inclusive condemnation of modernity came to form part of the doctrinal heritage of the Church. Successive pontiffs did not fail to make periodical references to that fundamental judgment in order to guide Catholic attitudes to secular life. It is sufficient to cite as examples the *Lettre aux archéveques et eveques francais* (1910) in which Pius X condemned the Sillon; the encyclical *Pacem Dei munus* (1920) of Benedict XV; the encyclical *Quas primas* (1925) of Pius XI; and *Summi pontificatus* (1939) and the broadcasts on Christian civilisation which emanated from Pius XII during the second World War. The set of concepts revealed in such texts not only implied a negative assessment of the modern world but largely supported the Catholic condemnation of a history which was an autonomous human achievement and of an independent human quest for the most appropriate form of collective life. This gave rise to a long period of enmity between Church and society. It also supplied those who ran the Church with their alibi for silence on the most tragic event of the times—the holocaust. It also allowed the Church to expect that human beings who had been led astray and had rejected the Church's authority would follow the right way of social life which only the papacy was able to show them.

Translated by J. G. Cumming

Notes

1. J. J. Gaume, *La Révolution. Recherches historiques sur l'origine et la propagation du mal en Europe* (Paris 1856), p. 12.

2. *Cf.* the explicit reference to Gaume in M. Lefebvre, *Ils l'ont découronné. Du libéralisme a l'apostasie. La tragédie conciliaire* (Escurolles 1987), p. 29. See also an example of the persistence of the notion in P. Calliari, *1789. Révolte contre Dieu* (Paris 1986).

3. G. Audisio, *Della società politica e religiosa rispetto al secolo decimono* (Florence 1876), pp. 184–187. On the evaluation of the Revolution by liberal Catholics, see: *Les catholiques libéraux au XIXe siècle* (Grenoble 1974).

4. On this aspect see D. Menozzi, 'La chiesa e la storia. Una dimesnsione della critianità da Leone XIII al Vaticano II', in *Cristianesimo nella storia* 5 (1984), pp. 69–106.

5. M. N. S. Guillon, *Collection générale des brefs et instructions de notre très-saint père le pape Pie VI*, I (Paris 1798), pp. 129–132.

6. *Ibid.*, II, pp. 574–582.

7. There are some indications in D. Menozzi, 'Tra riforma e restaurazione. Dalla crisi della società cristiana al mito della critianità medievale (1758–1848)', in *Storia d'Italia, Annali* 9. *La chiesa e il potere politico* (Turin 1986), pp. 769–806.

8. J. Godechot, *La contre-Révolution. Doctrine et action. 1789–1804* (Paris 1961), pp. 46–55.

9. On the origins of this idea, see: M. Defourneaux, 'Complot maçonnique et complot jésuitique', in *Annales historiques de la révolution française* 37 (1965), pp. 170–186. *Cf.*, in general, J. Herrero, *Les orígenes del pensamiento reaccionario español* (Madrid 1973).

10. B. Baczko, 'Le complot vandale', in *Le temps de la réflexion* 4 (1983), pp. 204–206.

11. L. Pasztor, 'Un capitolo della storia della diplomazia pontificia. La missione di Giuseppe Albani a Vienna prima del trattato di Tolentino', in *Archivum historiae pontificae* 1 (1963), pp. 299–341.

12. L. G. A. de Bonald, 'Théorie du pouvoir politique et religieux', in *Oeuvres complètes*, XIV (Paris 1843), pp. 243–245 and 274–280.

13. Novalis, *Werke, Tagebücher und Briefe Friedrich von Hardenbergs*, ed. H. J. Mähl, II (Munich & Vienna 1978), pp. 732–735.

14. R. F. Rohrbacher, *Tableau des principales conversions qui ont lieu parmi les protestants depuis le commencement du XIXe siècle* (Paris 1827).

15. A. Foa, *Gli intransigenti, la Riforma e la Rivoluzione Francese* (L'Aquila 1975).

16. G. Alberigo, 'Dal bastone alla misericordia. Il magistero nel cattolicesimo contemporaneo', in *Cristianesimo nella storia* 2 (1981), pp. 487–521.

17. D. Menozzi, 'Intorno alle origini del mito della critianità', in *Cristianesimo nella storia* 5 (1984), pp. 560–561.

18. *Acta Gregorii papae XVI*, I (Rome 1901), pp. 169–174.

19. *Pii IX pontificis maximi acta*, I (Graz 1971), pp. 198–223.

20. G. Miccoli, *Fra mito della cristianità e secolarizzazione* (Casale Monferrato 1985).

21. See the evidence in *Conciliorum oecumenicorum decreta*, eds. G. Alberigo et al. (Bologna 3/1973), pp. 802–816; *cf.* an example of their importance in H. J. Pottmeyer, *Unfehlbarkeit und Souveränität. Die päpstliche Unfehlbarkeit im System der Ultramontanen Ekklesiologie* (Mainz 1975).

PART III

The Legacy of the Revolution in Contemporary Christianity

Peter Eicher

Revolution and Church Reform: Ecclesiastical Power after the French Revolution

'Such a phenomenon in the history of mankind will never be forgotten'
(I. Kant)

1. The question of power

IN REMEMBERING the French Revolution of 200 years ago the Church comes face to face with the question of power. For this Revolution showed the world even more clearly than the Reformation how the Church itself exercises political power. The long-term result of the radical changes brought about by the French Revolution in the relationship between the power of the state and that of the Church is the separation in principle of Church and state which put the specific freedom of both as well as their relationship to one another on a new basis: the Church's opportunity for political influence was, in the wake of the French Revolution, separated from *state* action and was recognised in principle as *social* action (whether the state is in favour of the Church's social action or not). This meant, however, that the Church's attempt at being able to exercise state power itself was forcibly ended: from now on it had to learn to understand itself in its secular function as being a social force itself *in* the state.

After the French Revolution, the Church, as a part of society, was subject to the *civil* constitution of the state. The party of the Civil Constitution of the Clergy, which had emerged from the Gallican state-Church position, in 1790 still monarchistic in outlook, since 1792 more radically democratic, achieved, because of that, a permanent victory over the party of a 'clerical constitution of state power'.[1] The history of the Revolution shows that those still faithful to Rome and refusing to accept a civil constitution, saw the legitimacy of political action as being only guaranteed in a monarchical constitution whose divine right could again only be conferred by the Church in the *sacre*, in the consecration of the king. On the other hand, the representatives of the civil constitution, since 1792 anti-monarchical in outlook, were confident that the task of the Church was just as compatible with the freedoms founded on *human rights*, as with the *republican* commitment which, in 1795, demanded that 'the totality of French citizens' be recognised as the sovereign power and that 'obedience to the laws of the republic' be shown. As is well-known, this was rounded off with lasting success by Napoleon's consular Constitution of 1799 which demanded of the clergy the 'promise of loyalty to the constitution'.[2]

This question as to how ecclesiastical power should be incorporated into the democratically defined social structure, a question which, in the French Revolution, had not only torn the Church apart but also the nation within itself, has been settled as far as the Church also is concerned, most recently since the Second Vatican Council: as citizens of a state, all Christians are 'by conscience bound in obedience' to the legitimate power of that state, and, in fact, for the very reason that 'the political community and the Church, each in its own territory, are independent of one another and autonomous'.[3] In its long-term political effects, the French Revolution has overcome not only the Gallican state-Church position but every other form of Catholic state religion as well, and has thereby made an important contribution to the Church's reflection on its own task of proclaiming the Gospel in society. By doing so, it has done the Church an ever greater service than it has done to the power of the state which has since then found itself open to the difficulty of establishing the validity of its constitutions from within itself.

If the spiritual autonomy of the Church can be gratefully acknowledged by Christians as a result of the great Revolution, then, however, this independence of Church and state, achieved with difficulty in democratic constitutions, also includes today a task which the result of the bourgeois revolution continues to set the Catholic Church in particular.

For the democratic revolutionising of all political action faces the Church as a social body of importance with the question as to the institutional form of the exercise of power peculiar to it, that is of its own constitution and form of government. The fundamental de-sanctification of political action and all that legitimised that action, achieved in the French Revolution—in spite of all the actual re-sanctification of nation, people and constitution—faces the Catholic Church's monarchical and hierarchical form of constitution itself with the unsettled and burning question of its humanity. For, since the French Revolution, the appeal to 'divine right' in order to legitimise the internal exercise of power has been discredited. Once the legality of the monarchy's appeal to the *ius divinum* has been broken, then the representatives of the Church's exercise of power, that is the quasi-monarchical pope and the hierarchical clergy, are faced with the problem as to how they can substantiate theologically and politically their appeal to a divine authorisation of the exercise of *internal* power in the Church. The French Revolution compels a practical reflection on the *humanity of ecclesiastical power* with which it institutionally organises the task peculiar to it, namely the proclamation of God's rule in the world. The present commemoration of the French Revolution therefore invites the Roman Catholic Church to reform its internal exercise of power. It is a suitable moment to de-mystify the appeal of Church office-bearers to a divine secret in order to substantiate privileges of power in the Church which are only all too human, and, in doing so, to open the gate to thoroughly revolutionary Church reform. This I propose to justify and to give concrete examples of, both theologically and historically in the following, after first recalling two great historical-theological interpretations of the relationship between revolution and religion.

2. The historical-theological identifications

If there is anything that gives the idealistic expression 'modern times' a historical meaning, then it is the break which the French Revolution signifies for the new basis of action in bourgeois society. Because the liberation from the oppressive privileges of the nobility and clergy and the new substantiation of political action in the rights of freedom belonging to all human beings demanded by the Revolution, brought the fact irrevocably to light that for modern society the meaning of temporal and therefore historical action itself had changed. The French Revolution had, of course, like the English revolutions and the American declaration of human rights, not only extended old privileges to larger sections of society, but had detached the meaning of public action from what had legitimised it in the past and placed it on a new basis, on the *right* of free action for every human being.

Whether, along with Georges Sorel and Marxist-Leninist historiography, one interprets this right to free action as progress towards capitalist means of production and therefore claims to find 'the basic cause of this triumph in the economy',[4] or whether, along with present-day liberal research,[5] one seeks to understand the causes and motives of revolutionary action by means of a far more complex process of population growth and an increase in traffic movement, of changes in ways of thinking and radical social changes, of agrarian, industrial and social revolution, there still remains the need to explain the revolutionary *discontinuity* of action. For there is no question that, according to the way the revolutionary masses and their leaders saw themselves, likewise their reactionary and regressive critics—in spite of the continuation of a wide variety of old orders identified by Toqueville[6]—the Revolution brought forth a new subject of action: the subject who himself makes his own history in bourgeois society. The times are seen to be new by a bourgeoisie which bases its action on the constitutionally postulated right of all human beings to be free to determine what their history should be. For theology, which confronts all human action with the ecclesiastically proclaimed justice of God, it is surely not at the same time advisable to restrict the really revolutionary action to the bourgeois-reforming renewals of the years 1789–92 and in doing so too neglect the Terror under the Committee of Public Safety in 1793–94, likewise the transition to the property-owning republic under the Directory, as being the Revolution's *faux pas*; or, vice versa, to dismiss the Revolution wholesale because of the Terror. Instead it is just this novelty that theology should consider: namely that the citizens have, by their own right, both economically, politically and by military-revolutionary action, worked themselves through to a position of being the subjects of their own history, to a history of which 'terror' is also a part. In this respect it is not enough for theology to play off the reformers of 1789 against the regicides, Jacobins and sans-culottes in the years after 1792, or conversely, to turn the Napoleonic Empire as end-product of the Revolution against its origin. Theology must understand what the real political, social and economic action of the revolutionary bourgeoisie means *sub specie evangelii*. This understanding is quite basically crucial to theology's relationship with the modern age as a whole.

Together with the familiar traditionalist approach there are two great liberal answers to the question as to what the revolution means for Christianity in the modern age. Both answers, which try to bring the revolutionary enquiry vis-à-vis the Catholic Church under this concept, identify a historical greatness with God's revelation: the classic French historiography of J. Michelet identified the revolutionary action of the French people with the revelation of divine justice; G. W. F. Hegel's philosophy of history identified it with the realisation of God's freedom in history itself. If I put particular emphasis in what follows on this bourgeois theology of revolution, then I do so only because the opposing traditionalist political theology (that of Burke, de Maistre, the younger Lamenais, de Bonald, von Haller, Stahl, the elder Görres and Archbishop Lefevbre today) is easily seen through as the bad identification of God's will with the politically reactionary intent of its authors themselves[7] and will not be discussed again here. Because they identify the rules of the past with God's present, they themselves become the property of the past.

(a) The revelation of justice

When Jules Michelet brought the French Revolution to life again in a work of unparalleled narrative drama,[8] he did this in his capacity as incumbent of the chair of history and moral philosophy at the Collège de France: his history of the Revolution sets out to give back to a France laid low by the restoration (of the bourgeois monarchy of 1830, the weak Second Republic of 1848 and the Empire of 1852) as well as to the states of Europe pressing for liberation, the morality of the spirit which entered the world in the first phase of the Revolution. In those 'sacred days of the world' there arose for him 'the sun of justice', because the Revolution 'was in principle nothing other than the triumph of right, the resurrection of justice and the late reaction of the idea to brutal force'.[9]

Because Michelet took not only history but also the truth of Christianity more seriously than the theologians of his time, the question as to whether the new justice was identical with the Christian way of life or not was for him the decisive question of the history of the Revolution itself: 'historically and logically'[10] the question as to whether the Revolution was Christian or anti-Christian takes precedence over all others. 'Historically' it precedes them, because like no other it moved and impelled the Revolution's contemporaries, and 'logically', because only with reference to it can the legitimacy of the revolutionary novelty be discussed and proved. For Michelet, the Revolution poses the question, decisive for history and for Christianity, 'as to whether the dogma of grace and salvation in Christ, that is to say, the sole basis of Christianity, is compatible with justice, and whether it will continue to exist'.[11]

The answer turns out to be unambiguous. Christian enthusiasts who see the Revolution of 1789–92 as the fulfilment of Christianity must interpret the whole struggle of the eighteenth century against the spirit of the Church, as well as the real struggles on the streets of the Revolution, as mock battles, as a battle merely within Christianity. In doing so, however, they misunderstand the core of Christian dogma which lies in the doctrine of

God's free choosing of sinful man—and they misunderstand the spirit of the Revolution which, according to the spirit of the Enlightenment, bases the rights of all people on the *idea* of universal justice. The novelty of the Revolution can no longer only be understood as the (secularised) inheritance of the old, because the revolutionary demand for the brotherhood of all human beings builds only on the love of one person for another, in the same way as the rights of human beings are justified by their humanity. On the other hand, conditions in Christendom as it really is—in the Augustinianism of the Reformation no less than in the Council of Trent—can only be justified by God's free election to grace and they remain therefore with reference to a political and social order which is the incarnation of this divine granting of grace. Whether one stands in the grace of king and clergy or falls into disgrace in their eyes, decides on life and death in the *ancien régime*. As historian of France in the late Middle Ages, Michelet knew what he was talking about and it was easy for him to set against the lament for those killed in the Revolution the great lament for the victims of the Christian Inquisition, of witch burning and of religious wars.

So, according to Michelet—and H. Arendt will follow him in this[12]—the sum-total of the Revolution was in no way a liberation from oppressive forms of the *ancien régime*, it is not simple negation of the old Christian way of life, but rather the autonomous creation of a new *justification of freedom*. There are 'two principles, two spirits, the old and the new'[13] confronting one another in a revolutionary manner, no longer capable of being reconciled in a historical manner. Michelet therefore found reconciliation not in the old Christianity but in the universal religion of love, revealed in the revolutionary process as the religion of justice. It was the French *people* that Michelet celebrated as the revealing subject of this totally new religion, a people he was now able to identify simply with *la France*. It is the people of the Revolution who complete the Enlightenment of the eighteenth century, through, in fact, their belief in justice, that is to say, through the creation of the new religion of the bourgeoisie. And so, in spite of his historical-philosophical identifications, Michelet still came to the conclusion that the bourgeois religion[14] could no longer be reconciled with the old Christianity as such .His interpretation of the Revolution faces the old Church with the question as to its justice—and the bourgeoisie with the question as to the absence of grace in its historical praxis.

(b) The dawn of freedom

For G. W. F. Hegel 'world historical'[15] event of the French Revolution is the prerequisite for a truly philosophical understanding of history *per se*.[16] To him, the French Revolution is the event in which 'man stands on his head, *i.e.* on his thought, and builds reality accordingly'[17]: only through this Revolution has reality become rational, because only through it has the freedom of all human beings as a right and therefore as the foundation and purpose of society and state reached political recognition. And so for Hegel, the event of the French Revolution can only be understood by a philosophy identical with the understanding of the history of freedom itself. But the history of freedom is for Hegel the history of God Himself, the self-revelation of the *truth* of freedom.

If Hegel also shares with Michelet the view that something new came into world history with the Revolution, then, contrary to Michelet, it is precisely with the truth of Christianity that he substantiates this new epoch of freedom. The external reason for this is simply that Michelet comes from Catholic France; Hegel, however, from Protestant Prussia. Viewed at a deeper level, they are divided by a completely different conception of Christianity: if for Michelet it is the religion of the arbitrary order of grace, then for Hegel it is the 'religion of freedom'.[18] For Hegel, what the *Reformation* had brought to the light of consciousness only became practical in the *Catholic* France of the Revolution: namely through the free self-relinquishing of God in Jesus Christ, man has also been reconciled with himself, and that means with his freedom. For Hegel, therefore, the Revolution is indeed a 'glorious sunrise',[19] but it was preceded by the rising of 'the all-transfiguring sun'[20] of the Reformation which, with its light, had brought man to his inwardness *i.e.* to the awareness of his subjective rights. What the Reformation was for belief, the Revolution was for society and the state.

For Hegel, the Revolution was only possible and necessary in France because its 'government . . . was Catholic'.[21] For the unfree Catholic *form* of Christianity contradicts its *content* (*i.e.* God's freedom itself)[22] and thus sets believers at variance with the institution of the hierarchical Church and the sacredly legitimised arbitrariness of the princes. Because God's truth, in the Catholic Church, is imparted by individuals, by priests, Christian freedom remains external and therefore ultimately foreign to the people who are bound to servile obedience. Catholic man therefore remains at variance with himself and with the world. The Reformation, on the other hand, granted everyone the dignity, the freedom of which God was not afraid in Himself, to develop in himself or herself, that is really to believe *oneself*. Thereby, however, it reconciles the Christian citizen with his secularity and with the state: with the secularity of marriage and work, because man as a servant is free, and with the state, because as a free man he can give obedience to the state. In Germany, therefore, one found 'the

Enlightenment on the side of theology; in France it immediately directed itself against the Church'[23] which sanctioned the unheard-of injustice of the economy of privileges and the arbitrary behaviour of the state. A revolution without a reformation would therefore, for Hegel, be a simple 'stupidity of the modern age'.[24] And therefore the demand for human justice in the Catholic form of Christianity, and with that the abolition of the Catholic hierarchy, belonged, according to Hegel, to the unsatisfied demands of the French Revolution: the revolution remains unsatisfied without the reformation of the Roman Catholic Church.

These historical-theological arguments must however be distinguished from Hegel's empirical observations on the historical driving forces and political consequences of the French Revolution. These lie not in religious motives, but—as his *Philosophy of Law*[25] demonstrates—in the rise of the modern industrial worker society. Because in that society the individual can only satisfy his need to be a human being by his own work, he therefore steps out of the sacred bonds of tradition in order to base his rights in bourgeois *society* on his own work. Because however in modern production conditions this work leads to unequal classes (and to the dependency of colonies),[26] the *state* has to confront society based on the division of labour with its (the state's) demand for rights and morality. In this post-revolutionary society therefore, the functions also now befitting religion is the internalising of the rights and morality of the state for the citizens of this competitive society.

Hegel therefore invests the establishing of human rights in the French Revolution with an emphatic religious-philosophical solemnity (because their recognition is equated with the realisation of God's freedom) which does not however stop him explaining their historical accomplishment as a corollary to industrialisation and capitalist society. In doing that, however, the message of reconciliation serves to legitimise the industrialised competitive society which Hegel considers rational. It goes without saying that at the same time he is devastatingly critical of the dictatorship of the Committee of Public Safety which, according to Karl Marx, served 'with its mighty hammer blows to make the feudal ruins vanish as though from off the soil of France'.[27] Hegel did not take into consideration the violence of bourgeois society and the suffering of its victims—even if he was able to condemn, in an almost reforming spirit, the debasing *form* of Catholic truth and the misery of the laity treated like sheep by the clergy.

(c) The new empirical sober approach

'The' French Revolution does not exist: it is not a solid block. One must distinguish the chain of events, which for ten years filled the period of revolution on very different levels and with sharp internal splits, from the meaning given to it by its actors and their historians. Because the human beings who are actively and passively involved in a history never know what history they are making, so the meaning of the French Revolution also cannot simply be drawn from the newspapers and the propaganda of the time (the Abbé Grégoire and Pius VI saw it very differently). Likewise, one must distinguish clearly between the *motives* of those acting in a revolutionary way and the long-term *causes* of their action. To which one must add that the writers of history and above all the philosophers of history can never finally separate their analyses from the interests with which they themselves make their 'history'.

When Michelet celebrates the liberation from the old religion of grace and formation of belief in the new religion of universal justice as the central event of the French Revolution, he does not only give voice to the sources (which indeed he does) but still more to his hope for the religion of the people, the nation and mankind, of which he dreams in a still very Eurocentric manner. And when Hegel, in complete contrast, sees in this Revolution the political realisation of freedom which the Reformation had taught as being the liberation of man to his moral independence, then on both occasions he betrays the religious-philosophical imperialism which forces world history to be subordinate to the idea of God's history of freedom. And yet Michelet's belief and Hegel's idea are at least as good as the Marxist *idée fixe* of the smashing of feudalism in favour of bourgeois capitalism,[28] in grasping moments which characterised the historical consciousness *of* the Revolution no less than the motives of individual participants *in* the Revolution itself. In all this, as little has been decided about the long-term causes (Enlightenment, the Jansenist quarrel, Gallicanism, abuse of privileges by nobility and clergy, France's economic backwardness, the example of English parliamentarianism etc.) as about the direct reasons (failed harvests, the demands of the Third Estate, the King's political foolishness etc.).

But it is not these self-evident truths which today forbid an equation of the historical-philosophical visions about the great Revolution with its reality, it is rather the vast investigation by the social sciences of the institutions, the economic, social and political conditions as well as the religious and liberal ways of thinking during the Revolution *and* under the *ancien régime*, which nowadays leads to a new empirical sober approach and to care in dealing with the 'meaning' of the Revolution. As recent research however shows,[29] religion as always has a right to a key role in this, at least as far as the change in ways of thinking and the liberation *from* the traditional understanding of governing and social structure are concerned. Three facts taken as examples show that present-day research—from a socio-historical point of view—does not defuse the lasting questions for the hierarchical constitution of the Catholic Church, but makes them now genuinely humanly understandable:

—The demand for total freedom of *public opinion* which, in a speech to the National Convention (August 1791) Robespierre extolled as a human right consecrated by nature, also in matters of 'morality, law-giving, politics and religion',[30] achieves an unforgettable profile through detailed knowledge of the censorship which from 1750–80 was carried out by the theology professors at the Sorbonne with nationwide effect. Condemned at that time, in the name 'of our sacred dogmas' and 'the healthy theology which is entirely enclosed within Holy Scripture and venerable tradition',[31] were not only writings of Rousseau and Montesquieu, but also, even in 1780, the 'Histoire naturelle' by Buffon, because its conception of the age of the earth contradicted the literal sense of the text in the Book of Genesis. But at the same time, as present research shows, in the years after 1750 'public opinion' rose to become a real political power which neither clergy nor king could suppress: *vox populi, vox dei* became the slogan of the time.[32]

—Stereotypes of a uniform Catholicism under the pre-revolutionary clergy of France believed to have been destroyed by the Revolution and countered by the completely new cult of the Supreme Being of Reason, such stereotypes are themselves completely destroyed. Investigation into the wide variety in Catholic ways of thinking, rites, symbols and ideas of dogma among country-people, town-dwellers and Catholic intellectuals in the eighteenth century,[33] shows that republican Catholicism as well as the civil religion itself emerged from (Jansenist, enlightened and oppositional) Catholicism.

—Finally, investigations into de-christianisation before and after the Revolution[34] show that, with regional variations, people began as early as 1750 to dissociate themselves from ecclesiastical practices on quite a large scale; it was on this that the Jacobin de-christianisation, brought about by agitation and military means, was, to a large extent, able to count. The religious geography of France, which to the present day determines the pastoral situation and also the voting behaviour of the French, was thereby determined even before the Revolution.

3. The parable for the Church

Theology does not sit in God's council and can therefore not act as referee over history. But it must, with all the means of human reason, consider what God's history, borne witness to in the Bible, means for its public and private action. And so it must, in the first instance, apply the action of the Church itself to God's history which moves the world. For that we need to make a distinction in principle, to identify a biblical assurance and to spell out the structural change long overdue in the hierarchical Church.

(a) God's history and our histories

The Gospel of the old and the renewed covenant is not directed at human beings in an abstract way; rather it places Israel, and through Israel all nations, under the promise and the judgment of God's faithful action in His covenant. The Church, which has to bear witness to the world as to how God makes His history through His covenant, cannot itself steal quietly away out of the histories in which God Himself has become involved, with a benevolence extending to the death of His son on the cross. Because theology has to place the confusing histories created by nations themselves in the light of the living truth of God's action, it cannot be critical and careful enough in its dealings with the revolutionary events which, according to the historical understanding of contemporaries, renewed time itself. It goes without saying that, in doing so, theology is in no way empowered to celebrate the political meaning of a nation's history as being the revelation for world history.

For God's action can only be perceived through belief. Because God acts through His own word which, in the history of the crucified and risen Lord, overcomes 'every rule and every authority and power' (1 Cor. 15:24), the Lord's purpose cannot also be worked out from human histories themselves: it is revealed only in every new hearing of God's word. Theology is therefore prevented from making any historical-philosophical generalisations about God's action and likewise with the opposite identification, that of the politically manufactured meaning of our histories with God's revelation itself. The Christian community can therefore in no way make the French Revolution or any other history into the affair of God Himself. It can strip the revelatory character from the idealised images of history and the nationalistic patterns of interpretation, as well as from the traditionalist condemnations of this Revolution, and let them be seen as what at least they also are: images of the political will to power. When Michelet takes the justice in which the people have placed their revolutionary hopes, and when Hegel does likewise with the 'freedom' realised in this Revolution, and when both create from these a principle to judge world history and to make an idea intended as identical with God, then the Christian community must indeed denounce the illusionary nature of such theologies of history, but it must all the more participate in the real struggle of the people for justice and freedom.

For the Church is itself deeply *involved* in human histories, their expectations of meaning and their illusions. And in fact, not only because it competes with the other powers of this age in its own secular and therefore very concrete political power, but also because the Gospel to which it bears witness is what really reveals the human obligation of its own action: the Church then is the place where God's word sits in judgment in the world. Its solidarity with human histories is founded in this vicarial recognition of human guilt before God and the vicarial acceptance of the promise of the revolutionary history of God's covenant with the nations. Only in the power of His word does it stand in freedom also *against* the action in which it is involved. Its freedom is the freedom of God's word in action, of Jesus Christ who, as crucified and risen, has been lifted up as the living Lord of our histories until the end of our time.

If both are excluded, the *identification* of the historical meaning of the French Revolution with God's revelation and the *generalisation* of God's Word into a principle with which the Revolution can be judged by the Church, then surely the histories of mankind and also the French Revolution can be perceived in belief as being a parable of the movement of the world by the risen Lord of history. For if God through His covenant moves the world and not only the Church, and if the Church has to bear witness to the promise of this moving of the world by the God of the world, then it is exactly the revolutionary change in political conditions which can be recognised as a sign of God's rule in the world. It is a sign which demands a thoroughly revolutionary change in the still semi-feudal conditions in the Catholic Church's exercise of power, a sign that invites us today to demand the overdue reform of the hierarchical Church constitution with a thoroughly revolutionary strength.

(b) God's 'revolutionary' action

The word 'revolution' gained its historical meaning only when it became associated with the hope, founded in human rights, for a renewal of the political, social and legal constitution of France in the years 1789–99. If God's action, borne witness to in the Bible, is characterised as 'revolutionary',[35] then, in order to keep at bay all projections and historical-philosophical identifications, it must be restricted to the meaning revealed by God's history in Jesus Christ Himself. But in that, the renewal of all human conditions in the simultaneous revolutionary change of past, present and future becomes clear:

—In the death of Jesus Christ, according to the witness of the New Testament, 'We know that our old self was crucified with him so that the sinful body might be destroyed, and we might no longer be enslaved to sin' (Rom. 6:6f.). The true ally in covenant of God and mankind has, through His self-devotion even unto death, freed the Jews and all nations from the curse of sin by taking this curse upon Himself. *This* renewal of the covenant, in which sinful and godless man is reconciled with God, reveals in a revolutionary way the power with which man, in deadly fashion, rules himself and others: the power of death. This power, which first provides human histories with their drama and hopelessness, was broken by the reconciliation on the Cross, it belongs to the past. The recognition of mankind's breach of covenant, the critical awareness of the henceforth outdated deadly powers and freedom with regard to one's own *past*, no longer permit any divine justification of human history, nor any theological justification of political, social and ecclesiastical conditions, because, from now on, their guilty character can be recognised. This freedom to recognise guilt makes human conditions in every way open to revolutionary change.

—By the raising of Jesus from the kingdom of death, God gives the *present* its living Lord. With the elevation of the crucified Jesus as Lord of history, God justifies His own covenant of life for historical time. This revolutionary establishment of His rule contradicts the curse of human histories in a good way: it limits the power of their own laws and empowers nations to a life based on justice. 'He has showed you, O man, what is good;/and what does the Lord require of you/but to do justice, and to love kindness,/and to walk humbly with your God' (Mic. 6:8). After the raising of Jesus, prophetic witness is no longer a mere *demand*: now through His Gospel word, the Lord of history exercises in the present the justice which was prophetically promised. And Christians themselves must bear witness to this revolutionary action of God to their own present time.

—The rule of Jesus Christ places limits on our historical time. It is limited by the promise of the kingdom whose justice will put an end to our injustices. Christians can therefore neither fear revolutionary change in structures of state as being the end of the world, nor can they view them with hope as being the arrival of the kingdom of justice. Hope in the coming of Jesus Christ makes relative the revolutions of our histories by bearing them as signs of the limits placed on the world by the *coming* Lord of history.

Because the powers of this historical time are reconciled with God, because they are subordinate to the just and merciful rule of the risen crucified Jesus and because they are open to God's future with the world, the internal power of the Church can therefore be changed in a revolutionary way, according to the parable of political revolution. The French Revolution has made its contribution to that. What are Christian communities doing for that today?

(c) The time has come

The paradox is clear: nobody wishes to see a return to the ecclesiastical conditions which the French Revolution so violently destroyed. And with the exception of some schismatic traditionalists, nobody in the Church longs to return to a clerical tutelage of the state or even to Church states. And yet today the basic structures of the *ancien régime* and of the feudal privileges of the clergy are still internal characteristics, in a centralised and bureaucratically modernised form, of the inner constitution of the Roman Catholic Church. The freedom of democratically based action, which the Church also demands today of the state, is denied within the Church. The human rights which Pius XII sought to obtain from totalitarian states in order to maintain ecclesiastical freedoms and which John Paul II decreed as having their origin in Christian tradition, these rights are denied almost all Christians in the Church, all women and all lay people. As the injustices and lack of freedom in the hierarchical constitution of today's Roman Catholic Church are known in detail to readers of *Concilium*, it is not necessary to list them here again. But they need to be seen in the light of the political parable which the French Revolution represents for this Church today.

The knot of history cannot for ever remain so unresolved that Christians as *state citizens* perceive for themselves the rights which the Revolution fought for and which the Church in the meantime blessed, but as *citizens of the coming Kingdom of God* they remain subject to a Church constitution which clings to nothing other than a past order of the world. Two hundred years after the Revolution the time has come to put an end to this lack of simultaneity and to think for once that revolutionary action can be justified in changing the Church too. In conclusion, I shall name the reasons for this which all Christians know, but which still have no effect, because apparently nothing in the world is more difficult than changing the religiously legitimised but thoroughly secular power structures in the Church of God:

—The political and social rights of all mankind are *validated* for the Church not because of their revolutionary justification but out of the awareness of God's justice, borne witness to in the Bible; but this difference in justification does not diminish, but rather increase the *right* of all Christians to equality of active and passive rights in the Church. Women and married men have the *right* to free access to all ecclesiastical offices. And they have the *right* to fight for this access in conflict with the hierarchical Church leadership. And because the exclusion from ecclesiastical offices of almost all those baptised offends God's justice and leaves countless congregations without leadership, Catholic Christians have the *duty* to abolish the present disorder in the Church.

—There can and must be just as little legitimisation of the democratic orders of state and society by divine right, as of aristocratic and monarchical orders. But that means also that the hierarchical-centralist form of the Roman Catholic Church is incapable of any theological justification[36]: this form of administering power, taken over historically by the clergy using the model of European power-structures (of the ancient Roman, Germanic, medieval-feudal and modern age absolutist and present-day bureaucratic-centralist kind) is also totally historically relative and open to change. The Churches of the non-European world have not only a right to the autonomous development of Church structures according to their traditions, but also the duty to seek out that Church structure which does justice to their social and political context. Here too, it is not a principle of freedom and justice which can lead the Church, but only energetic action in renewed listening to the word of God which will give courage to the small revolutions in the Church. The democratic choice of bishops and priests in no way contradicts their calling by the word of God alone, nor their mission on which the Church sends them. But the appointment of bishops by the Vatican with power-political aims against the dioceses, the secret diplomacy of the nunciatures and those appointed by the Vatican by-passing local churches, these do contradict not only the meaning of justice but also the meaning of ecclesiastical power itself. Surely that is only there to proclaim the rule of the risen crucified Lord at this time in the world. To plead that his or her revolutionary action will create order in the Church is the right beginning of revolutionary action for a Christian person.

—The Church today rightly takes action on the principle of freedom in public opinion in those states which still suppress this quite central demand of the bourgeois revolution. But even if it has to be recognised that *decisions* on the validity of laws and the delimitation of dogma must be made in the Church, then there must also be a recognition that public opinion, the *sensus fidelium*, develops perfectly well its strict criteria of decision-making. Without the freedom of public opinion in theology and in congregations, the decisions of the magisterium remain arbitrary—the same arbitrariness of the *ancien régime* which Michelet though the Revolution had removed from the world.

—It is part of the history of the French Revolution's influence—a clumsy reaction to it—that the infallibility of the pope, one hundred years after the revolution, incorporated absolutist features into the papacy's form of government, understandable anyway only in a monarchical sense. The hope remains that the interpretation given this by the German bishops in 1875 and accepted in Rome will have itself a revolutionary effect: it was stated that this means nothing other than that the infallible magisterium remains 'bound to the content of Holy Scripture and tradition'.[37] For tradition can only again be the interpretation of the Gospel of the Old and New Testaments, a Gospel which itself bears witness to the Judge and Last Word on ecclesiastical traditions.

Hope for reform in the Church does not lie in remembering the French Revolution. But the French Revolution gives those in the Church who hope a parable for the revolutionary changes in which the Church also cannot remain uninvolved.

Translated by Gordon Wood

Notes

1. This re-evaluation of the Civil Constitution of the Clergy, as is taken for granted in recent Catholic historiography, goes back in France to the empirical renewal of the history of religion of the French Revolution by A. Aulard, *Le culte de la Raison et de l'Etre suprême* (Paris 1892); by the same author, *La Révolution française et le régime féodal* (Paris 1919); A. Mathiez, *Les origines des cultes révolutionnaires* (Paris 1904); by the same author, *Contributions à l'histoire religieuse de la Révolution française* (Paris 1907); by the same author, *La Révolution et l'Eglise* (Paris 1910); by the same author, *Rome et le clergé français sous la Constituante* (Paris 1911); by the same author, *La question religieuse sous la Révolution française* (Paris 1929); and G. Lefebvre, *La Révolution française* (Paris 1968). In Germany, it goes back to W. Gurian, *Die politischen und sozialen Ideen des französischen Katholizismus* 1789/1914 (Moenchengladbach 1929). For present-day Catholic evaluation see R. Aubert, *Die katholische Kirche und die Revolution*: H. Jedin (ed.) *Handbuch der Kirchengeschichte*, vol. VI/1 (Freiburg, Basel, Vienna, 1971), pp. 3–104; on the recent historiography of religious movements in the French Revolution see B. Plongeron, 'Le fait religieux dans l'histoire de la Révolution française' in *Annales hist. de la Rév. franç.* 47 (1975), pp. 95–133; on individual points see below notes 29–34.

2. Proofs in W. Gurian, *op. cit.*, pp. 33–40.

3. *Gaudium et spes* No. 74 and 76.

4. G. Sorel, *Über die Gewalt* (Frankfurt a.M. 1981), p. 103; on the Marxist-Leninist account which devotes much space to religious-political questions see W. Markov, A. Soboul, *1789 Die Große Revolution der Franzosen* (Berlin 1973).

5. See, together with studies on the Revolution in the journal *'Annales' (Economies. Sociétés. Civilisations)*, particularly F. Furet, D. Richet, *Die Französische Revolution* (Frankfurt a.M. 1968); by the same author, *La Révolution*, 2 vols. (Paris 1965–66); and the account by W. Mager *Frankreich vom Ancien Régime*

zur Moderne (Stuttgart 1980). For an overview of the history of research see E. Schmitt, *Einführung in die Geschichte der Französischen Revolution* (Munich 1976).

6. See A. de Tocqueville, *L'Ancien Régime et la Révolution*(Paris 1856); *Der alte Staat und die Revolution* (Munich 1978).

7. Nor does the legitimisation of 'Christian parties' in present-day Europe, by deriving it from the republican forces of Christianity unleashed by the French Revolution, escape such identifications; on this justification of 'Christian politics' see H. Maier, *Revolution und Kirche* (Munich 1973).

8. J. Michelet, *Geschichte der französischen Revolution*, 10 vols. (Hamburg 1929/30)—1st ed. *Histoire de la Révolution française*, 7 vols. (Paris 1847–53); quoted in the following notes in the French edition in 3 vols. (Paris 1901–03).

9. 'Ce sont les jours sacrés du monde', *op cit.* (Préface de 1847), p. liv; 'le soleil de la justice', *ibid.*, p. xlix; 'La révolution, qui n'était dans son principe que le triomphe du droit, la résurrection de la justice, la réaction tardive de l'idée contre la force brutale . . .', *ibid.*, p. xlviii.

10. 'Cette question, historiquement, logiquement, précède tout autre', *op. cit.* (Introduction), p. i.

11. 'Et ce débat . . ., n'est pas moins que la question de savoir si le dogme de la Grace et du salut par le Christ, seule base du christianisme, est conciliable avec la Justice, de savoir si ce dogme est juste, de savoir s'il subsistera', *op. cit.* (Introduction), p. iii.

12. H. Arendt, *Über die Revolution* (Munich 1963), pp. 33–42 (E.T. *On Revolution*, (New York 1963).

13. J. Michelet, *Histoire*, *op. cit.* (Introduction), p. iv: 'deux principes, deux esprits, l'ancien, le nouveau'.

14. On the concept of bourgeois religion see P. Eicher, *Bürgerliche Religion, Eine theologische Kritik* (Munich, 1983); by the same author, 'Le Christ selon les penseurs de la société civile bourgeoise' in *Rev. des scienc. phil. et théol.* 66 (1982), pp. 199–224; on the discussion of modern understanding of revelation see by the same author, *Offenbarung—Prinzip neuzeitlicher Theologie* (Munich 1978).

15. G. W. F. Hegel, *Vorlesungen über die Philosophie der Geschichte*, Theorie-Werkausgabe, vol. 12 (Frankfurt a.M. 1970), p. 535; quoted in the following notes as *Phil. d. Gesch.*

16. See J. Ritter, *Hegel und die französische Revolution* (Frankfurt a.M. 1965).

17. *Phil. d. Gesch.*, *op. cit.*, p. 529.

18. *Vorlesungen über die Philosophie der Religion II*, Theorie-Werkausgabe, vol. 17 (Frankfurt a.M. 1969), pp. 203f. and *passim*.

19. *Phil. d. Gesch.*, *op. cit.*, p. 529.

20. *Ibid.*, p. 491.

21. *Ibid.*, p. 529.

22. See on this and the following: *Enzyklopädie der philosophischen Wissenschaften III*, Theorie-Werkausgabe (Frankfurt a.M. 1970), pp. 355–361; on Hegel's interpretation of Reformation and Revolution see L. Oeing-Hanhoff, *Hegels Deutung der Reformation: Hegel, L'esprit objectif—l'unité de l'histoire* (Lille 1970),

pp. 239–257; by the same author, *Die Kirche—Institution christlicher Freiheit?*: J. Ratzinger (ed.) *Dienst an der Einheit* (Düsseldorf 1978), pp. 105-132; on the theological discussion of the problem of freedom see Th. Pröpper *Erlösungsglaube und Freiheitsgeschichte* (Munich 1988).

23. *Phil. d. Gesch.*, *op. cit.*, p. 526.

24. *Enzyklopädie*, *op cit.*, p. 360.

25. See particularly the preface and the section on bourgeois society and the state (§ 189–360) in the *Grundlinien der Philosophie des Rechts*, Theorie-Werkausgabe, vol. 3 (Frankfurt a.M. 1970), pp. 11–28, 339–512.

26. See *ibid.*, p. 392 (§ 248, additional remark).

27. K. Marx: *Marx-Engels-Werke*, vol. 4, p. 339; on Hegel's criticism see the famous section 'Die absolute Freiheit und der Schrecken' in the *Phänomenologie des Geistes*, Theorie-Werkausgabe, vol. 3 (Frankfurt a.M. 1970), pp. 431–441.

28. On this critique see F. Furet Penser, *La Révolution française* (Paris 1978).

29. See overview in B. Plongeron, *Le fait religieux*, *op. cit.* (Note 1, above).

30. M. Robespierre, '*Habt ihr eine Revolution ohne Revolution gewollt?*' (Leipzig 1958), pp. 132–155.

31. Quoted in M. Perronet, 'Les censures de la Sorbonne au XVIIIe siècle' in F. Lebrun, R. Dupuy (ed.) *La résistance à la Révolution* (Rennes 1986), pp. 27–35, 29; on Buffon, see 32.

32. See e.g. K. M. Baker, 'Politique et opinion publique sous l'Ancien Régime'. S. Maza 'Le Tribunal de la nation: les mémoires judiciaires (1770–1789)' in *Annales* 42 (1987), pp. 41–89.

33. See G. Le Bras, *Études de la sociologie religieuse*, 2 vols. (Paris 1955–56); B. Plongeron, *Théologie et politique au siècle des Lumières* (1770–1820) (Geneva 1973); *La vie quotidienne du clergé français au XVIIIe siècle* (Paris 1974) (Lit.).

34. See M. Vovelle, 'Étude quantitative de la déchristianisation', in *Dix-huitième siècle* 5 (1973), pp. 163–172; *Religion et Révolution* (Paris 1976).

35. On the theological talk of 'God's Revolution' see F.-W. Marquardt, *Theologie und Sozialismus* (Munich, Mainz 1985), pp. 124ff., 145–149.

36. See P. Eicher, 'Hierarchie' in *Neues Handbuch theologischer Grundbegriffe*, vol. 2 (Munich 1984), pp. 177–196.

37. DS 3116.

Pierre Colin

How Can We Speak about the 'Christian' Themes of the Revolution?

I RECENTLY came across an early twentieth century history textbook by some Catholics which presented the French Revolution without even mentioning the Declaration of Human and Civic Rights.[1] Nowadays human rights tend to be seen as one of the main themes of the Revolution; certainly they appear to be the theme which attracts the widest consensus, both nationally and internationally. The consensus is not complete, however. There is difficulty in settling on a list of rights, and in any case the list has grown considerably since 1789. There is more or less hidden disagreement which emerges when it is seen how the question of the basis of human rights is posed, or avoided. Above all there is the often rhetorical nature of discourse from politicians who are not really bound by it.

The position of the Catholics is both favourable and delicate. They are favourably placed because they are well-provided with religious and philosophical resources for grounding human rights on an idea of man, but delicately placed because they must give a proper explanation of the prolonged opposition to the *1789 Principles* by the ecclesiastical hierarchy and numerous Catholics. However we interpret this opposition, the turning-point found in *Pacem in terris* does seem to have been made possible by a change in historical awareness. The fact that human rights had their origin in the Revolution became obscured as history did its work, so they could be freed of their individualistic connotation and be given a foundation quite different from classical liberalism.

But the Bicentenary is rewakening historical memories and inspiring studies of the ideological background which led to the declaration of liberty and equality in 1789. And this is raising all sorts of questions once again. Can we still be satisfied with the argument that human rights spring from a Christian tradition distorted by eighteenth century philosophical rationalism? Even with a less simple view of the 1789 background, is it really a 'Revolutionary theme' that Catholics are seeing as Christian when they now consider defence of human rights to be a basic requirement of Christianity? And underlying these questions there is an even more difficult one. Whether as process, as myth or as idea, it is revolution itself, in the new meaning that what happened in France gave to the word, which is the most specific theme of the Revolution. And the question of whether or not the goal of fundamental and voluntary transformation of society can meaningfully be seen as Christian will not be solved merely by talking about Christians' disliking violence.

1. A difficult problem

Attempting to formulate the problems these questions involve is like being caught in a whirlwind of preliminary difficulties. These I will arrange in two series.

(a) What revolutionary themes are we discussing?

There are three possibilities here. First, the themes which preceded the French Revolution and prepared the way for it by providing it with ideological capital. Secondly, the themes which emerged from the actual process and development of the Revolution. Thirdly, the themes which were an outcome of the Revolution and which later history has incorporated, with changes, into our institutions and ways of thinking.

Study of the first or second of these groups of themes would force us into assessing the part actually played in the Revolution by ideas, either old or new. The third group fits our topic better, since it directs us to the inner complexity of the inheritance left by the Revolution. Within this complex inheritance there are at least two lines that we shall be following: how the achievements of the Revolution were taken up into the republican idea; and how past and future, memory and goal, combine in the idea of revolution.

(b) The significance of calling some revolutionary themes 'Christian'

Who calls these themes 'Christian', and in the name of what? We can approach these questions from two points of view, that of historical provenance, and that of judging their Christian authenticity.

Marcel Gauchet has recently renewed the historical provenance aspect of the question in his book *Le désenchantment du monde*.[2] He presents Christianity as 'the religion of the exit from religion', an expression which rapidly became famous. It implies that contemporary society is structurally detached from religion, and that Christianity made the separation possible. Gauchet's argument rests on an original methodology that sees Christian— or Christic—monotheism as introducing a structured set of 'historically possible futures' which actual history in its contingency has exploited in diverse ways. An important point here—leaving aside the debate we have had with him elsewhere[3]—is that Marcel Gauchet thus connects to the Christian system not only the centuries of Christendom but also contemporary society, which is structurally outside the religion that made its existence possible. So we have to distinguish two phases in the development of the Christian possible futures. Before 1700 or so, 'the major components of modernity were in a phase of gestation within the development of religion; at about that date, we tip over into their phase of fulfilment through being outside religion'. (p. 322).

To illustrate the point we may take the example of the revolutionary theme of the nation as one and indivisible. In its way this theme takes up the Christian symbolism of the 'mystical body', which had already been transposed from Church to Kingdom within the framework of the modern territorial state. The question is what this borrowing of the symbol means when we approach it from the point of view of judging its Christian authenticity.

Marcel Gauchet's conceptual reconstruction does not trespass on the theologians' domain; it is for them, using their own norms, to judge the historical products of a Christianity they sometimes find disconcerting. From the theological point of view, some elements in the history of the influence of Christianity can make it seem like a history of uncertain deviation, or indeed of disfigurement or counterfeit. But the counterpart of these reservations is that theologians are always tempted to credit to their individual Christianity even things which were originally condemned by their own ecclesiastical tradition. This may be a 'reclamation' strategy; counterbalancing it is the unfettered proliferation of Christianity, not always along the ways of orthodoxy even as represented by the diversity of confessions. The theologian may, however, have good reasons for giving his blessing after the event to things come to fruition outside the Churches, or outside his Church. How can he not recognise the value of reason enriched by Christianity, when his respect for natural reason has allowed theology to incorporate a whole philosophical and juridical tradition from Greece and Rome in the course of its development?

It must be said that this incorporation of the Greco-Roman inheritance complicates the problem extraordinarily. To begin with, the intellectual capital which Christain thought has drawn on in its theological judgments at the different stages of its history becomes extremely complex. How do references to revelation and references to reason combine? Next, and more important, the Greco-Roman inheritance, which was transmitted through Christian tradition, is always liable to be taken up in itself and for its own sake. This has indeed happened, in the returns to antiquity that punctuate our history in the West. This has led to a tangle of ambiguity which the question of natural law demonstrates clearly.

In order to deal with the new problems posed by the enlargement of the world, the sixteenth-century scholastics made use of ancient and medieval resources. Their work was taken up in its turn by the papal texts which elaborate the social teachings of the Church from Leo XIII on. And *Rerum novarum* presented natural law as a fundamental element in 'Christian philosophy'. But which natural law? Seventeenth and eighteenth-century jurists meanwhile had elaborated the concept anew, against the background of modern political philosophy. Is it not their idea of natural law that underlies the 1789 Declaration? Much later however, when John XXIII took up the question of human rights, he did so in the light of what his predecessors had said about natural law. Is it really the same idea at work in the two areas? If there are two ideas, is one Christian and the other not? Or are they both Christian, but in different respects?

Unquestionably the debate about Christian themes of the Revolution involves the norms and criteria of theological judgment. In particular the question raised is that of the status granted by theology to natural reason, and especially its capacity for historical innovation.

2. The Republican inheritance of 1789

At the time of the first centenary of the French Revolution in 1889, the country was divided; a lay and republican France faced the old Catholic and monarchical France. The young Republic celebrated itself as it celebrated a Revolution the benefits of which were listed in school textbooks. According to Paul Bert in *L'Instruction civique à l'école*,[4] we owe to the Revolution the cult of France, of national unity, justice, the rights and duties of the citizen, the sovereignty of the people, regular and honest administration, taxation voted by the citizens and, summing it all up, liberty, equality and fraternity (pp. 133–134).

Since the Second World War if not before, there has been a broad consensus in France about the republican institutions, with Catholics in agreement, by and large. To what extent though does this assent to the institution imply adherence to the republican spirit which Alain defined in 1901 as 'the cult of reason'?[5] Not all the republicans of that time would be prepared to consider the Revolution as a single 'block', to use Clémenceau's term. No more would republicans today. To celebrate 1789 is not to ratify 1793, and the process which led to the Terror is under constant re-examination, so far without being fully elucidated. But the bases on which there is agreement concerning the Republic have been brought out by Claude Nicolet in *L'Idée républicaine en France*,[6] a major work which traces the history of the idea: 'Ultimately, the two aspects of the Revolution to which republican tradition has always been unanimous in laying claim wholly and unreservedly are the 1789 Declaration of Rights on the one hand, and the schemes for education and civic instruction on the other' (p. 113).

Now, the two major points in the republican consensus are also the two major points of nineteenth-century Catholic opposition to the *1789 Principles*. One may wonder if the conjunction of the two themes does not indicate how difficult it is to unite the two age-old French traditions, liberal and jacobin. Be that as it may, the fact remains that Catholic opposition did occur, even if it came mainly from the hierarchy and did not meet with the approval of all French Catholics. Today, it is hard to see how a French Catholic could claim to be republican in spirit without thinking about this business, its mark is still so strong. Were he to try to ignore it, others would take it on themselves to remind him of it, and rightly so.

The brief *Quod Aliquantum* with which in 1791 Pius VI opened the series of papal condemnations of freedom of conscience was not merely a response to immediate circumstances; it condemned the philosophy of the century, in the name of which attempts were being made to establish among men an untrammeled liberty and equality, which smothered reason completely. What was needed was to establish liberty and equality in their true nature, rather than restricting them. The theme of intellectual freedom was not unknown to theological tradition; for Thomas Aquinas it was fulfilled in the opening of the intellect to the first truth, which is God, and in the consent of the will to the Absolute Good, which is God.

But this metaphysical discourse about (personal) liberty does not lead to modern discourse about (public) liberties. How can this modern freedom 'to think, say, write and even print in religious matters everything the most disordered imagination can suggest' be tolerated? Two things forbid it. First, the sinfulness of human free will, subject as it always is to the most grievous aberrations. And secondly, the idea of a Christian society, which must not deprive this fallible liberty of the public support it needs.

As Paul Ricoeur has shown in his article 'Liberté' in the *Encyclopedia universalis*, separation of the two discourses on freedom, the metaphysical and the political, is a general feature of the modern period. They will only be reunited again with Kant, and especially Hegel. But is there at least a hint of this reunion in liberal Catholicism? In 1830, *L'Avenir* was fighting for a union between God and Liberty, which had been separated by the alliance of Catholicism and despotism. As used here, the word 'liberty' certainly includes the set of public liberties demand for which is connected with the inheritance of the Revolution. In historical fact, however, the *Prospectus* for the launch of the journal spoke of 'the indestructible need for freedom which is specific to Christian nations'. And on the theoretical level, in an article dated 16 October 1830, Lamennais wrote that without the Christian principle, which alone could found it in law, liberty was merely fact, and as such was subject to all the vicissitudes of history.[7] Extending the text, it is as if the modern thinking on civil and political liberties had to be reworked and justified in the light of a Christian philosophy of the freedom of the human person. And Lamennais was well aware that he was defining a 'new liberalism' which conflicted with that of contemporary liberals.

While conceding nothing to doctrinal liberalism, Lamennais considered in 1830 that the play of liberties gave the Church the chance to regain its spiritual audience, so acutely needed by society. She should of course first defend her own liberty, especially in the educational field. But should she also seek to maintain, or regain, her official privilege within the state? The logic of the positions adopted led to a revision of the usual views. So the way was opened which would lead to what Charles de Montalembert called 'a free Church within a free State'.

In retrospect, the difficult transition from confessional state to lay state emerges as one of the major concerns of the post-revolutionary age. It was all the more divisive in that, for a long time, both sides remained convinced that if the Church lost its dominant position in France, it would also lose its spiritual power. Are we today better able to pass Christian judgment on the theme of the laicity of the state? The historical source of this problem, as of others, is of no help in solving it. Following Marcel Gauchet's thesis would lead us into a demonstration of the Christian presuppositions behind the modern theme. Was the separation of religious and political not originally a result of the spread of Christianity in the Roman Empire? And though they were to recombine in the Christian Empire, they did so in a hierarchically ordered form and kept a distinction between spiritual and temporal which prepared the way for later developments.

The consequences drawn by the moderns, however, can be clearly seen in Auguste Comte. The distinction between temporal and spiritual power must be maintained, but the latter should be secularised. A thorough investigation of the problem of the laicity probably involves considering the moral responsibility which the lay State attributes to itself, especially when it takes over the moral education of the young. In this respect, the end of the nineteenth century is still an exceptional observation post. The republican school system challenged the dogmatism of the Church head on when it avowed the intention of forming a 'freedom of thought'—a rational independence of judgment—distinct from mere 'freedom of conscience'.[8]

The problem of education is still a very sensitive area, but French Catholics were not slow to call for and welcome the Vatican II declaration *Dignitatis humanae*. There is to be a colloquium at the Institut Catholique in Paris in March 1989 on this very topic of the in-depth change which has made possible assent to human rights and religious freedom. Our working hypothesis is that this assent is now possible as a result of the Church looking anew at society, and doubtless also at itself.

Marcel Gauchet's expression describing society as structurally free of religion is open to question. To the extent that the civil authority separated itself from the institutions of the Church, religion has indeed become a private matter. But within our society there is also public debate, on ethical as well as strictly political questions. Provided they accept the principle of pluralism, there is nothing to stop Christians taking part in this public debate both as Christians and in their capacity as Christians.

Ultimately, the theme of the laicity brings us face to face with an underlying question. Using the term with the meaning Paul Valadier gives it in his book *L'Eglise en procès*,[9] can we recognise the Christian value of this 'society in debate', which is not in the direct line of descent from the French Revolution but has some share in its inheritance?

3. The idea of revolution

If one accepts that the Revolution itself should be considered as a revolutionary theme, then the subject I agreed to deal with leads naturally to the following question: in what way and to what extent can the theme of revolutionary change in society be said to be Christian?

But I must first define the scope of my discussion. There are a large number of 'revolutionary' movements in the world today, each differentiated by its aim and ideological resources but also by the political situation of the country where it occurs and the nature of its revolutionary action. How far are these movements a result of the situations, such as famine and extreme poverty, which have always led to revolt? Which of these struggles are causally connected with human rights? Which are for the right of freedom of expression, against regimes which forbid democratic debate; for socio-economic rights, against governments which tolerate or organise injustice, exploitation and social exclusion? For the right of peoples to shape their own lives, against the old colonial situations? These questions are not exhaustive. But when one is examining a particular revolutionary movement and asking whether it is legitimate for Christians to take part in it, the situation must be looked at individually. This would exceed both my remit and my competence. I shall therefore confine myself to following the development of the idea of revolution against the French background.

Ought we perhaps to call it the idea—or myth—of the Revolution? At any rate we shall be working with the new meaning the French Revolution gave the word, that of an absolute event, which makes a radical break between *before* and *after*; which is the end of what now becomes the *ancien régime*, and the starting-point of a new world.

How are we to make sense of the fact that this absolute event was drawn out over time? The question of the end of the Revolution was dividing the revolutionaries as early as the end of 1791, when the Girondins and the Montagnards were in disagreement over whether achievements to date should be consolidated, and exported, or whether the process of the Revolution should be pursued in even more radical ways. There is a certain similarity between this disagreement and that which divided the republicans who were in power, from the socialists, at the end of the nineteenth century. For the latter, the Republic was simply a step towards the social Revolution, which had yet to come. Thus for Jaurès, as François Furet emphasises, the jacobin saga of which he was writing the history was 'the herald of a liberation which would be more decisive for humanity'.[10]

Despite the quite startling telescoping of history by republican school textbooks which sing the benefits brought by the Revolution—a Revolution which produced the citizen with the whole set of civil and political liberties—they are not unaware that it took a hundred years, and more revolutions, for this achievement to pass fully into effect. But in France at least, the Third Republic marked the end of the Revolution, and the advances which still remained to be made would be brought about within the legal framework of the Republic. As Claude Nicolet writes (*op. cit.*, p. 108): 'Revolutionary violence, which is permissible against any form of despotism, is no longer permissible against the Republic'.

We are thus dealing with two markedly different interpretations of the theme of revolution. The republican interpretation centres on the opposition between despotism and liberties. It accepts that in some other countries there remains a need for the struggle against despotism—or its contemporary equivalents such as military dictatorship or totalitarian government. But it justifies the struggle because its aim is the establishment or re-establishment of a real *de iure* State, the only institutional basis of respect for the liberty of the citizen and of equality before the law.

But this does not exhaust the dynamic of change set in motion by the proclamation of the rights of man. How did we get from rights as liberties, within the framework of law, to rights as entitlements or dues owed to the individual society, which imply a quite different role for the state? Without going into the history, let us point out that in part at least, this dynamic springs from the tension between the principle of liberty and the principle of equality (social as well as legal).

The second version of the theme of revolution is the one produced by the various forms of socialism. Marxism-Leninism was to set a decisive stamp on it. The Russian revolutionaries had the French Revolution constantly in mind, but after 1917 the Soviet Revolution became the model of social revolution.

Now, within the field of contemporary philosophy, there is a vigorous critique of the idea of revolution in the form which results from the cross-fertilisation of these two historical references. Inspired by the work of Solzhenitsyn, writers like Claude Lefort and Marcel Gauchet have challenged the totalitarian mirage of a completely unified society which has reached a definitive state of reconciliation with itself.[11] Similarly, François Furet has shown that in order to 'think' the French Revolution, the historian must break free of the image of it that we inherited from its makers and which still dominated classical historiography.[12] We thus have a process that starts with a critique of totalitarianism, goes back over French jacobinism, and finally criticises the idea of the Revolution for being 'secretly allied with a totalitarian image'.[13]

Such denunciation of a death-dealing delusion has no inherent connection with the counter-revolutionary theme of the satanic character of the French Revolution. Yet in the forms it takes today, revived by the approach of the Bicentenary, counter-revolutionary thought is not incapable of making use of the political philosophy just referred to.[14] On the contrary however, it may be thought, as I think myself, that if Christians are critical of this political philosophy, it will be because they have internalised not only the theme of personal human rights, but also the democratic theme of the human rights of the citizen. Many Catholics were slow to accept democracy, but it is Christians' attachment to it which may legitimately alert them to the suspicion of complicity with totalitarianism by which the idea of revolution is affected.

We are thus led to think about the attraction that the theme of revolution has had in Christian circles. To what extent was it a result of familiarity with the pattern of fundamental differentiation between *before* and *after*? Be that as it may, for a Christian this pattern evokes the temporal division effected by the coming of Christ: the abolition of the previous religious regime which becomes the *Old Testament*, and the setting up of the *New Covenant*. True, there are obvious differences. In the theme of revolution, only the break is stressed, and there is no parallel to the resumption of Judaism within Christianity which fulfils the promises of the old Covenant. Moreover, whatever the similarities, and the influences, a marked disparity emerges when the religious theme is projected onto the political field. But that is precisely the problem: does a real transposition occur, or is the political field invested by a theme which, though secularised, remains religious? At this point Raymond Aron's analysis of 'secular religions' and his use of the word 'millenarism' become relevant.

Historically, the word refers to the Christian heresies which pictured an earthly realisation of the Kingdom, at the end of time, as a preliminary to its heavenly fulfilment. In *Polémiques*,[15] Aron applies the term to a communist policy, 'which confers absolute value on an objective that can be reached in a finite time, or that confuses a historic society—built or to be built—with the ideal society which would fulfil the vocation of mankind' (p. 178).

The Christian progessivism of the 1950s is already well behind us, but it is relevant to our subject in so far as it fused eschatological horizons. As Fr Bigo wrote at the time, 'The earthly future, which communism seems to open up to mankind, is starting to be thought of and lived by some Christians as its eternal future'.[16] This kind of criticism is relevant at its own level, and also bears on some religious components of the myth of revolution. But if it is adequately to solve the problem of whether the theme of revolution is 'Christian'—positively, on the level of history, or negatively on that of theological judgment—the theme would have to be fundamentally connected with millenarism. Is it so connected?

Here we must turn to Emmanuel Mounier, the founder of *Esprit*, who in his *Manifeste au service du personnalisme*[17] launched the rallying-cry of a 'personalist and community revolution'. He was later to have doubts about using the word 'revolution', being disturbed by its seeming direct call to violence. He retained the word, however, firstly to show that it was a *fundamental* change that had to be made: the civilisation which must be created was new, totally distinct both from bourgeois civilisation and marxist society; and secondly, to show the *voluntarist* nature of a plan of action: men must think out the new society they want to see, but then bring it into existence.

By what means, and within what foreseeable time-limits? Mounier, no millenarist, was not aiming for the violence which would suddenly replace one society by another. The revolution—spiritual, economic and political—he was calling for was to be a collective work of long duration. Experience has proved him right. His retention of the word 'revolution' is nevertheless significant, from both the human and the Christian points of view: ultimately, it implies a rejection of fatality. The true revolutionary movement is perhaps the one which leads human beings to regain their individual and collective power of decision so that they may become as fully as possible the subjects of their own history. Whatever the cultural and/or religious origin of this desire for responsible freedom, and even if one accepts that the libertarian conscience of modern man developed through opposition to Christian institutions, how can the desire for responsible freedom not be shared today by the disciples of Christ?

Translated by Ruth Murphy

Notes

1. *Histoire de France*, cours moyen illustré, par une réunion de professeurs Mame-Poussielgue.
2. (NRF 1985).
3. *Un monde désenchanté?* Debate with M. Gauchet. Under the direction of P. Colin and O. Mongin (Cerf 1988).
4. (Paris 1882).
5. 'Le culte de la raison comme fondement de la République' in *Revue de Métaphysique et de Morale* (1901), pp. 112–118.
6. (NRF 1982).
7. *L'Avenir*, introduction and notes by G. Verucci (Rome 1967), pp. 4 and 10.
8. See C. Nicolet, *op. cit.*, and 'L'idée républicaine plus que la laïcité' *Le Supplement* (April 1988) pp. 45–52.
9. (Calmann-Lévy 1987).
10. *Esprit* (Sept. 1976), p. 176.
11. See C. Lefort, *Un homme en trop* (Seuil 1976) and M. Gauchet in *Esprit* (July-Aug. 1976).
12. *Penser la Révolution française* (NRF 1978).
13. C. Lefort, *Esprit* (Sept. 1976), p. 207.
14. See J. Dumont, *Pourquoi nous ne célébrerons pas 1789* (A.R.G.E. 1987), p. 7.
15. (NRF 1955).
16. *Le Progressisme*, aspects doctrinaux, (Spes 1955), p. 6.
17. (Aubier 1936).

Bernard Quelquejeu

Acceptance of the Rights of Man, Disregard for the 'Rights of Christians': The Inconsistency of Rome

A striking contrast

TO ALL who have become aware of it and who begin to study it with some attentiveness, a contradiction exists which gives reason for astonishment: the contrast between the Roman Church's present commitment to respect for and encouragement of the liberties and rights of man, in the civil, social and political spheres, and the Roman authorities' inability to respect and encourage liberty within the Church itself.

The commitment of the Church authorities to the liberties and values proclaimed by the French Revolution is today a fact which any observer must recognise, for it is well known that this has not always been the case. The acceptance by the Roman Church of the civil, social and political doctrine of the rights of man—according to the Church's own understanding of them, a point which will be more fully considered later—dates from the 1960s: Pope John XXIII's Encyclical *Pacem in terris* (1963) and the Declaration *Dignitatis humanae* on religious liberty, promulgated on 7 December 1965 by the Second Vatican Council. The consistent, radical condemnation by papal authority, between 1789 and 1965, of 'modern liberties', starting with freedom of opinion and of conscience, is a well-known fact, recalled in several articles in this present issue of *Concilium*.

Since 1965 it would not be difficult to call to mind declarations or initiatives which clearly reveal the commitment of the Roman pontiff to the defence and encouragement of the rights of man in society: Paul VI's address to the United Nations in 1965 implicitly recognising the ideal proclaimed in the 1948 Universal Declaration of Human Rights; the creation of the Papal Commission 'Justice and Peace' in 1967; the presence of representatives of the Holy See in a number of intern.~tional organisations and at such conferences as Helsinki or Belgrade; the theme chosen by the Roman Synod of 1971: 'Justice in the World'; etc.

If one bears in mind the 1965 acceptance of, and the subsequent resolute commitment to, modern rights and liberties within contemporary societies, one cannot fail to be surprised on seeing the incapability of the Roman Catholic authorities to recognise the implications of this change of attitude for its own institutional procedures, its internal lifestyle and customs, and even 'Catholic' mentality and culture. Surprised: the word is inadequate. It would be more accurate to say stupefied or even scandalised. To all appearances, having seen something of the ethical and political message of the French Revolution and the various traditional formulations of the rights of man and having decided to become their spokesman in the contemporary world, institutional Catholicism has refused to turn on itself the critical gaze which it directs towards other societies, as if it considered that this change of attitude had no implications whatsoever for itself.

This contrast between preaching in favour of liberties in the outside world and very strong resistance to any change in ecclesiastical customs and the institutional procedures of the Church in the direction of Christian liberty, certainly merits some attempt to explain it. Such flagrant inconsistency must, without any doubt, result from deeply hidden causes which relate to the very essence of a centuries-old institutional unconscious which continues to exert its influence even when the Church's self-image, at least on the surface, has been perceptibly modified. However, before putting forward some elements of an explanation, and indeed precisely to prepare the ground for their comprehension, it is necessary to concentrate for a moment on this inability to recognise and promote Christian liberty in the processes and mechanisms of ecclesiastical life and Christian morality.

A Church which disregards Christian liberty

Without making any claim to completeness, let us select, from among many others, as significant examples, a few observations and facts, chosen deliberately from different areas, which make clear this inability and this refusal. Let us study them in the light of a few New Testament texts which lead us into the rich perception of Christian liberty: 'The truth shall make you free [. . .] if the Son shall make you free, you shall be free indeed' (John

8:32 and 36). 'The Lord is the Spirit, and where the Spirit of the Lord is, there is liberty' (2 Cor. 3:17). 'Now we have been discharged from the law, having died to what held us captive, so that we serve in the newness of the Spirit and not in the oldness of the letter' (Rom. 7:6). 'You, brethren, have been called to liberty; only, do not use your liberty for an occasion to the flesh' (Gal. 5:13). 'Stand fast in the liberty with which Christ has set us free' (Gal. 5:1).

(a) The law relating to the faithful in the new Code of Canon Law

After many debates, and particularly those which accompanied the project, then the abandonment, of a *Lex ecclesiae fundamentalis*, a new Code of Canon Law was promulgated in 1983. It reveals a perceptible degree of progress in comparison with the Code of 1917: it gives the 'faithful' a central place; better still, it devotes a certain number of canons to the formulation of their rights: 'Obligations and rights of all the faithful' (c. 208–223), 'Obligations and rights of the faithful laity' (c. 224–231). It is only fair to underline a few of the formulations which show a certain degree of recognition of the progress of modern liberties: 'true equality of all the faithful, as regards their dignity and activity' (c. 208), 'the right and even at times the duty to state one's opinion on what relates to the well-being of the Church' (c. 212:3); the possibility 'of founding and organising freely charitable or benevolent associations' (c. 215); 'the right to be accorded in the earthly city the liberty which belongs to all citizens' (c. 227), etc.

But one must also point out the very strict limits of this timid advance along the road of Christian liberty, and this is seen in at least four aspects. First, it will be noted that the recognition in principle of certain rights is immediately hedged about with conditions for exercising them which considerably limit their effect. For example, in the practice of theology and sacred studies: 'the rightful freedom of research and of prudent expression in matters belonging to their competence, *whilst preserving the submission due to the magisterium of the Church*' (c. 218); or 'the right to state one's opinion on what relates to the well-being of the Church *whilst preserving the integrity of the faith and of morality and the reverence due to the holy Pastors*' (c. 212:3), etc.

Next, having examined the rights conceded to the faithful laity—the right to exercise the apostolate (c. 225, 229), the regular ministry of reader and acolyte, for men only and 'without payment by the Church' (c. 230:1), and the temporary mission of deputising for the priest in the ministry of the word, liturgical prayer, baptism, distribution of the Eucharist (c. 230:3), etc.—one must emphasise the extremely restricted nature of the rights thus conceded. All 'powers' remain, in reality, a clerical monopoly, a fact which makes a formality (*i.e.* of no effect) the equal dignity of all which is affirmed elsewhere, and allows the inegalitarian and clerical constitution of the Roman Church to survive almost intact.

Thirdly, it is sufficient to compare the list of those rights allowed by the Code with the liberties demanded by various Charters of Rights for Catholics published in the USA by the Association for the Rights of Catholics in the Church, in Germany by the *Christenrechte in der Kirche*, in France by *Droits et Libertés dans les Eglises*, to become aware of the distance which separates these timid canonical advances from those liberties and rights which Christians today, more or less everywhere, in the light of contemporary historical and theological research, judge it to be indispensable to confer on Catholic institutions in order to establish sufficiently the exercise of Christian liberty in the Church. In their judgment, the Church should incorporate, to become its true self, many modern liberties formulated in the spheres of law, morality, membership of institutions, politics, culture, and all this, of course, is based on the logic of its specific quality as an institution, that of 'communion'.

Finally, examination of the Code of Canon Law reveals one last deficiency: apart from the very vague canon 223:2, 'It is the responsibility of the ecclesiastical authorities to regulate the exercise of the rights of the faithful', and a few others, for instance the very restrictive procedure[1] for appeal in the case of disputed administrative decisions to the Second Section of the Apostolic Signature, one must note the absence of institutional guarantees for investigating disputed cases and ensuring respect for the law. This, however, is one of the most indispensable advances achieved by modern societies: one can only speak of an effective system of rights when a judicial power has been established endowed with sufficient autonomy and independence, including access to *ad hoc* appeal procedures and legitimate rights of appeal.

(*b*) *The code of procedure of the Sacred Congregation for the Doctrine of the Faith*

A second example of the Roman Church's inability to apply to itself, in its own internal life, the rules and criteria which it recommends other social or state organisations to respect, is provided by the regulations established by the Sacred Congregation for the Doctrine of the Faith for 'the examination of doctrines'. The name and the mode of operation of the 'Holy Office' were changed by the 'Motu proprio' *Integrae servandae* published by Pope Paul VI in 1965.[2] The internal regulations announced therein appeared six years later: this was the *Ratio agendi* for the examination of doctrines[3] signed by Cardinal Seper. A commentary by Mgr. Hamer, secretary to the Congregation, was later[4] to define the legitimate interpretation to be given to certain terms in the *Ratio agendi*.

These regulations provide for a long and very meticulous procedure described in 18 successive points. An attentive examination reveals that this procedure explicitly contradicts a substantial number of the inalienable rights universally recognised by contemporary societies as guarantees of a fair trial before an impartial tribunal.

Let us summarise briefly some of these neglected rights:

(i) No separation of the prosecuting and judicial authorities: it is the same authority which conducts the investigation, draws up the evidence of accusation and formulates the 'verdict'.

(ii) As regards the information provided about the investigation: the accused author is only informed that a case is being brought against him at the thirteenth stage of a procedure which has 18 stages. The following stages have already occurred, quite unknown to him: the initial examination (nos. 1–7) including the adoption if required of the extraordinary procedure (no. 1), the nomination of his representative *pro auctore* and of two expert assessors (nos. 2–4); then the examination before the tribunal of consultants (no. 8); the first judgment of the ordinary Congregation of the Cardinals of the Sacred Congregation (nos. 9 and 10); finally the papal hearing for approbation of the verdict (no. 11).

(iii) The choice of advocate: not only is the accused author unable to choose the representative *pro auctore* who is to defend him before the tribunal of consultants, but he will never know his identity. No advocate responsible for putting forward the rights of the defendant is present at the ordinary Congregation of Cardinals responsible for formulating the first judgment (nos. 9 and 10). Lastly the accused has neither the right to choose expert witnesses, nor that of being accompanied by an advocate at the possible 'interview' with delegates of the Sacred Congregation provided for in nos. 13 and 14.

(iv) Disclosure of documents: no disclosure to the accused of all the documents relating to the charges and the investigation will take place.

(v) The right of defence itself: the accused author is only invited to present his 'response' (no. 13) following an initial judgment already pronounced by the ordinary Congregation of Cardinals.

(vi) Publicity given to the proceedings: it is understandable that a certain degree of secrecy might be imposed in order to protect the reputation of the accused; however, there is no provision for any kind of monitoring to guarantee the impartiality of the judgment.

(vii) Double judgment by the same tribunal: the 'verdict' provided for in no. 15, subsequently pronounced by the Congregation, in fact constitutes a second judgment passed by the same tribunal on the same case.

(viii) Lastly, the right of appeal: there is no provision for any procedure or authorised body to allow for the possible exercise of any right of appeal.

Confronted with any criticism on these points, Mgr. Hamer would argue, in the commentary referred to earlier, that there is no question of a 'trial' in the civil sense of the term, and therefore that the legal guarantees universally recognised in this area in democratic societies have no claim to be respected here. Now, considering the personal and social consequences of 'opportune decisions' (no. 16) taken at the end of the examination, as they have been seen to occur in the cases of such theologians as H. Küng, J. Pohier, C. Curran, L. Boff and several others, it is legitimate to ask questions about the significance and the pertinence of this argument.

(c) The procedures and criteria for the appointment of bishops

If there is one area in which the historical experience of centuries of political despotism has forced the constitution-makers of 1789 and, subsequently, those of democratic societies to be scrupulously watchful and to provide rigorous guarantees of liberty, it is that of the choice of those who hold power. A complete organic doctrine of the limitation and balance of powers, the necessity of counterbalancing authorities, regular free elections, universal suffrage, public opinion, etc. is the outcome of these painful experiences.

One would search in vain, in the procedures for the choice and appointment of bishops, for any kind of reflection, within Christian institutions and the specific character of the constitution of the Church, of these results of modern experience. This is not the place to suggest what might and ought to be done in this direction in conformity with an authentic theology of the Church and its structural origins as a communion. At most it is timely to echo the chorus of lamentations arising today from every continent, on the subject of the policy of appointments pursued for several years with persistent determination, with the aim of modifying the composition of national episcopates. Not only—in opposition to the practices of the ancient Church—does the choice of new bishops not involve to the slightest extent the people of God in the diocese concerned; but, more astonishingly still, it involves less and less the respective episcopal conferences. Almost everywhere there has been a return to the pre-Conciliar practice according to which the appointment is prepared by the Nuncio and decided by Rome with no possibility of discussion. To all appearances the aim is to change the internal balance of national episcopates, to re-establish a universal episcopate and substitute for majorities which support the putting into effect of Vatican II, new majorities dominated by a more strongly dependent relationship to the central power of Rome. The case of Holland, where the process has been completed, is well known; that of Austria, still in progress, is equally so. Many other examples exist.

If it is true that Christian liberty can only develop and grow by inspiring a synergism of communion within the Church any threatened reduction or alteration of the dynamic of communion, to the advantage of the conformities of submission and the over-simplifications of subjection, is a direct menace to liberty. In few areas can the Roman institution's visceral refusal to apply to itself procedural norms originating from the ethic of the rights of man which it enthusiastically urges on groups, societies and states outside itself be seen with more force and clarity.

(d) The elaboration of Catholic 'moral doctrine'

A fourth example of the Roman Church's inability to accept, in its internal practices, the consequences of its recognition of modern rights and liberties, is provided by the exercise of its magisterial authority in the elaboration of what it calls its 'moral doctrine'.

The examples are numerous and recent enough for us to be content here with a brief reminder. One will recall first of all the long process of reflection undertaken at the instigation of John XXIII, then Paul VI from 1963 onwards, of which the dramatic outcome was *Humanae vitae* (25 July 1968). This case is exemplary, for it demonstrates in detail the real way of working of the central Roman power, in a kind of physiology of the ecclesiastical apparatus and its specific pathology. It brings on stage all the Church's actors: the laity (either individually or in their representative organisations), the various experts and specialists (demographers, doctors, sexologists, psychologists . . .), the moral and pastoral theologians, bishops, according to their several responsibilities, the papal commissions, the cardinals, the Council, the pope. We see in action, as the process moves upwards, the progressive elimination, first, of the faithful, systematically dispossessed of the right to express their opinion where moral doctrine is concerned, then of the experts, then the bishops, then the cardinals. The logic of this deprivation of powers is implacable: in 1964, Paul VI removed from the authority of the Council the question of birth control; finally the Holy Father was to decide alone, in diametrical opposition to the conclusions of the Papal Commission which he had himself first appointed and whose membership he had subsequently modified many times.

If it is objected that this is an issue which dates back to 20 years ago, one may simply refer to the recent history of *Donum vitae*, the Instruction of the Sacred Congregation for the Doctrine of the Faith of 22 February 1987, concerning respect for nascent human life and the dignity of procreation. Despite the affirmation, at the beginning of the text, that the Instruction is the product of a vast consultation, it is now known that the experts called to give evidence were carefully selected, that no account was taken of the opinion of numerous bishops, that Cardinal Ratzinger did not even consider it worthwhile to reply (in the last three months of 1986) to a proposition for a consultation emanating from the President of the International Federation of Catholic Universities, which are intimately concerned, however, because of their Catholic hospitals.

Comparison of the two cases reveals remarkable common elements and proves that we are dealing with a coherent and intractable attitude; there is nothing, at present, to suggest that it might even partially be re-examined or called into question.

The Roman Church's inability simply to *hear* the moral and Christian experience of the faithful leads to the negation of the right of the faithful to seek out and adopt, in the responsible freedom of their conscience, moral ways of behaviour involving either individual or collective life. The result is this startling gap between official positions concerning moral doctrine and the real state of the living consciences and the practices of millions of Christian men and women, a gap which in some places has attained the dramatic proportions of an abyss.

(e) *The place of women in the Church*

We shall refer finally to the major area of disagreement concerning the place allotted to women in the Roman Church. If there is one central affirmation of the tradition of the rights of man, it is certainly that of the equal dignity of every human being, of whatever race, sex, etc., and the various declarations of rights have all emphasised that all forms of discrimination based on sex were opposed to this radical equality—this includes the 'International Convention on the elimination of all forms of discrimination against women' adopted by the United Nations on 1 March 1980.

In fact, all the official documents by which the Holy See legitimates its refusal to re-examine the ecclesiastical status given to women, their participation in Church activities and the question of their access to the instituted or ordained ministries, present identical characteristics. Firstly, their arguments from theology or from tradition reveal curious gaps, to which we shall return at the end of this article. Next, they appear to attach no importance to the support which, viewed objectively, their attitude affords, in terms of social symbolism, to sexually-based discrimination practised elsewhere. Finally, they do not consider that this position constitutes in reality a form of discrimination which attacks the basic equality of human beings which they profess elsewhere in their commitment to the rights of man: they do not make this judgment because they do not even *see* the situation. It is precisely this blindness, strange as it is, which constitutes the problem and which requires, besides attempts at diagnosis, appropriate therapeutic action.

Let us end at this point this series of examples which illustrate the inconsistency between acceptance of the rights of man and the failure to recognise the 'rights of Christians' in the Roman Church. Let us hazard some elements of an explanation which mark out, provisionally, directions for research which need to be pursued.

Some attempts at an explanation

Such an obvious contradiction assuredly results from profound conditioning, from causes which act very powerfully and which are largely unknown to the participants themselves, from an institutional unconscious which has been deeply-rooted for centuries, and continues to produce its effects even when self-awareness, superficially at least, has changed to some extent.

(a) The Roman Church, guardian of a Christendom under threat

Historians, for their part, have not failed to put forward their hypotheses. According to them, the contradictory attitude of the Roman authorities is the result of many centuries of history.

The message of Jesus and the primitive Church had powerfully helped men to become conscious of the true dignity of the individual.[5] During the first three centuries of its history, the Christian Church ceaselessly claimed what we now call rights of conscience, for example against the claims of the imperial power. Writers like Tertullian, Lactantius, Hilary of Poitiers, echo enthusiastically the Gospel message of the liberty of conscience. From 313 AD the Latin Church was to find itself entrusted with the social and cultural leadership of the West. The consequences of this responsibility were to be immense. The rapid rise of apologists for the 'Christendom' which was coming to birth and for state violence in the service of doctrinal orthodoxy was witnessed. Bishops like Ambrose or Martin of Tours still refused such methods, Pope Leo I, in 385, approved the execution of the heretic Priscillian. The proclamation of the Gospel, of the 'truth which makes free' (John 8:32) was to give way to the establishment of Christendom, then, quite naturally, to its defence against everything that threatened it: which implied acceptance, at a very deep level, soon to be given its theoretical formulation, of the ideology of the established order. From this point of view, demands for the rights of the individual must inevitably appear subversive. Hardly a century before Vatican II, in 1864, Pius IX could not fail to condemn, without appeal, the freedom to choose freely one's religion (*Syllabus* no. 15, DZ 2915). To explain the contradiction between such a doctrine and *Pacem in Terris* it is not enough to invoke the legitimate reaction of the papacy to the militant liberalism of the nineteenth century: the language of anathema imposed itself literally on a Church heavily committed to the defence of a threatened Christendom.[6]

The profound nature of this inheritance, which is largely unconscious, may usefully shed light on the limits of the acceptance of 1965. Sufficient to realise that the rights of man are an instrument which can be used to expose the pathologies of social and political power in the outside world, this acceptance has still not been capable of modifying the Church's awareness of itself so that it may learn to *see* the diseases from which its own institutions suffer.

(b) Acceptance of the rights of man—but which ones?

The ideology of Christendom, of 'Christian civilisation', involves a politico-religious paralysis which carries within it the seeds of an anathema against the modern concept of the rights of man. Re-read the counter-revolutionary apologists:[7] if they emphasise so much the Catholic religion as 'dominant', it is because they are convinced that only religion—the genuine one, Catholic society—is capable of fulfilling, by perfecting it, civil society, which is in itself imperfect. For them, there can be no 'natural' without the 'social', any more than there can be a 'social' without the 'religious': the natural order, like the social one, can only find its legitimate fulfilment, political and metaphysical, in Christian religious order. And as the French Revolution, in its essential principle, separated the political and the metaphysical, there can only be a total incompatibility between the Roman Church and the doctrine of the rights of man.

Such was to be the 'thesis' of the Christian society: the Catholic Church has never thought in terms of nor allowed political liberalism. We refer readers on this point to J. Moussé's article in this current issue. It is certainly this governing thesis of political theology which has determined the fundamental attitude of successive popes. Even if, in response to pressure from modern societies, it has been necessary to admit the 'hypothesis' of the secularised society of the industrial era, this is destined to remain a hypothesis, as is shown by the encyclicals *Immortale Dei* (1885) on the Christian constitution of societies, and *Divini Redemptoris* (1937), in which Pius IX included this lapidary formula: 'Christian civilisation, the only truly human city'. Recent studies of the thought of John Paul II, as it may now be analysed in numerous spoken and written utterances, show that it is still, identically, the same thesis which dictates, covertly, the moral and political doctrine of the Roman Church.

The result of all this is that the Church's apparent acceptance of the tradition of the rights of man conceals, in reality, besides an attempt to recover its ideological balance, a very subtle process of doctrinal reinterpretation which considerably alters the genuine significance of the traditions deriving from the Enlightenment. Re-read from this viewpoint the declaration of the Council on religious liberty: why did it take such laborious discussions, such a long document, to enounce a principle which has appeared ever since the eighteenth century in every Declaration of Rights? Why does *Dignitatis humanae* multiply oratorical precautions, concessive restrictions, equivocal formulae (see nos. 13 and 14, and *passim*)? The theoretical displacement may be schematically summarised as follows: the right to religious liberty is ultimately founded on the 'nature' of man as interpreted by the Church's magisterium. It is thus that an inalienable and universal right, springing from the concept of man as having come of age and as master of his historical destiny, is shown, at the end of the Roman 'reconsideration', to lead to the obligation to adhere to the Catholic Church!

One must thus conclude that the 'Rights of Man' affirmed by the Roman Church by no means coincide on all points with the 'Rights of Man' in the tradition of the French Revolution or the American War of Independence. Therefore, what we have so far called Rome's inconsistency will seem less surprising, as it finally reveals itself as less inconsistent, perhaps, than it appeared at first sight.

(c) *The Church's obsession with safeguarding its institutions and with power*

A third direction for research is suggested by those analyses which reveal the phenomena inherent in all power-structures.

In general, any social group only ensures its minimal *social integration*, necessary to its historical survival, by secreting a representation of itself, its origins and legitimacy, which is termed as ideology. According to its own particular constitution, ideology in this sense will only *motivate* if it is *self-justifying*: it establishes the rightness of the group in being what it is and doing what it does. This is why it necessarily *simplifies*. Moreover, it is always, to a marked extent, *unconscious*: rather than an objectifiable concept, it is more an interpretative code in a dialectical relationship to an idealised self-image. Lastly, it has a specific characteristic of *inertia*, of delayed reaction, displaying symptoms, which are also specific, of intolerance (the reverse side of orthodoxy), self-enclosedness, and even blindness.[8]

These general characteristics, applicable to every human group, take on a specificity which accentuates their qualities if, when considering power-relationships, they are applied to the operation of an apparatus designed for domination. The ideology of such an apparatus will be self-justifying, and, to be so, must simplify, making use of simple motivating schematisations. It will often be tempted to distort reality or even to hide the threatening or intolerable aspects of reality. Moreover, there is no legitimation which is entirely transparent: one observes that there is an unawareness, a non-knowledge, of the exercise of power. Finally, it involves an inertia-effect, a sort of delaying or standstill effect, which is very striking: each power imitates and repeats some former power, even and especially when it has taken its place. Ritualising and stereotyping habitually have a dominant role here.

Having learned long since from historical experience and conscious of the immense sufferings which a single power, without institutional limitations, cannot fail to cause when driven by the strong forces of ideological motivation, men have devised a whole armoury of guarantees of various sorts to limit its power: division and separation of powers, establishment of counterbalancing forces, monitoring through public opinion and the freedom of the press, etc.: in short, the institutions of democracy, based on the doctrine of the liberties and rights of man.

Nothing of this kind exists in the Church of Rome. There, authority is still exercised in monarchical fashion, undivided, unregulated, with no counterbalancing forces, public opinion, or any possibility of legal action against the administration. Thus it is hardly astonishing that ideological phenomena have a particular virulence: auto-legitimation, authoritarianism, claims to infallibility, blindness and lack of awareness, predilection for secretiveness, tendency to inertia and stereotyping, traditionalism, fear of innovation. All these are characteristics which one cannot fail to recognise in is preoccupation with safeguarding its own institutional existence, in its repetitive obsession with its own magisterial authority.

Precisely because reference to modern liberties constitutes, through its historical origin, the foundation and legitimation of guarantees against tyrannical powers, it is more understandable that the Roman Church feels a very great ideological reluctance, which is largely unconscious, to apply to itself, to reveal and limit ecclesiastical despotism, a doctrine which today it recommends and promotes to combat despotism exercised by societies and states.

(d) Sexuality and power

'Certain official positions . . . are dependent on outdated concepts and perhaps also on a psychosis of celibate men without experience of this area of life', declared Maximos IV at the Second Vatican Council when, on 23 October 1964, it was learned that, by Papal decision, the question of birth control had been declared to be outside the Council's competence. It is in fact worth noting that the three subjects thus withdrawn (birth control, celibacy of priests, ordination of women) are all related to sexuality. The events relating to *Humanae Vitae*, recalled above, point in the same direction. Which subject produces such institutional paralysis, such a collective psychosis, such a tetany of the ecclesiastical apparatus? A question of dogma, relating to the knowledge of God, the confession of the faith, Christology, pneumatology? No: the lawfulness of a method of contraception . . . It is on a question of the normative regulation of sexual behaviour that the authority of Rome employs all its resources, and in what a way! Such an occurrence gives much food for thought. One must indeed come to the conclusion that for Rome, ultimately, it is its very power which is at stake. One finds oneself suspecting, with Maximos IV, that the exclusively masculine and celibate character of the Catholic clergy could well count for more than a little in this matter. And the fact that the crucial problem which is invoked every time is the 'irrevocable' nature of Roman doctrine is what allows one to suspect that the wish for omniscience, total power and infallibility which obsesses such an institutional apparatus, stems from the hidden but extremely close links which unite sexuality and power. These are all questions which cannot afford to wait to be re-examined for their own sake, with a view to the evangelical health and well-being of the Church's communion.

Conclusion: Christians are organising themselves to promote liberty in the Church

The preceding analyses lead to the conclusion that only a consistent long-term course of action, co-ordinated on an international scale, can in the end divert the direction of ecclesiastical customs and the institutional procedures of the Roman Church in the direction of Christian liberty. It would be a grave mistake to underestimate the weight of the obstacles which one must learn to measure and remove in order to make any significant progress.

This action has begun. Let us recall some of its recent stages. On 22 March 1975, a small group of theologians published in Paris, in *Le Monde*, a 'Manifesto of Christian Liberty', enouncing, after a brief preamble, some 15 fundamental rights deriving directly from Christian baptism. The following year a commentary on this Manifesto appeared.[9].

On 19 December 1979, in West Germany, a committee, *Christenrechte in der Kirche*, was established, which was rapidly organised into 22 regional committees. It defines itself as 'an ecumenical movement of Christians within the heart of the Church, joined together in order to realise the rights of Christians, to which we are led by the liberating message of Jesus Christ'. In May 1982 it presented to the Catholic bishops and the leaders of the German Evangelical Churches a Memorandum setting out the theological foundations of Christian rights and their relationship to the rights of man, emphasising that this is an essential question for the Church's credibility and reviewing briefly the categories of people who are under particular threat.

On 9 March 1980, in the USA, was founded the Association of Rights of Catholics in the Church (ARCC),[10] with the aim of 'introducing a collegial understanding of the Church, in which Catholics at all levels share in the decision-making process and effectively exercise their responsibilities' and 'to guarantee to each Catholic the basic rights which are rooted . . . in his baptism'. The ARCC published in October 1983 a 'Charter of Rights for Catholics in the Church', comprising 23 articles, the first draft of a future Charter on an international scale. In numerous countries (Holland, Switzerland, etc.) groups or associations have followed up this initiative and undertaken various activities of similar kinds. In France, the *Initiative Droits et Libertés dans les Eglises* (IDELE)[11] began its work at Pentecost 1981 and held a forum in Paris on 21–22 November 1987. These are the first steps of a long march.

Translated by L. H. Ginn

Notes

1. Patrick Valdrini, *Conflits et recours dans l'Eglise* (Strasbourg 1978).
2. Latin text in *Osservatore Romano*, 6–7 December 1965.
3. Latin text in *Osservatore Romano*, 5 February 1971.
4. *Cf. La Doctrine Catholique*, no. 1656, 16 June 1974.
5. See *e.g.* H. de Lubac, *Le drame de l'humanisme athée* (Paris 1959).

6. *Cf.* C. Wackenheim, 'The Theological Meaning of the Rights of Man', *Concilium* 124 (1979), pp. 49–56.

7. *Cf.* B. Plongeron, 'Anathema or Dialogue? Christian Reactions to Declarations of the Rights of Man in the United States and Europe in the Eighteenth Century', *Concilium* 124 (1979), pp. 39–47.

8. *Cf.* J. Ellul, 'Le rôle médiateur de l'idéologie', *Démythisation et idéologie*, Colloque Castelli (Paris 1973), pp. 335–354.

9. *Le Manifeste de la liberté chrétienne: Texte et commentaire* (Paris 1976).

10. ARCC, P.O. Box 912, Delran, New Jersey 08075, USA.

11. IDELE, 14 rue Saint-Benôt, 75006 Paris, France.

Pierre de Charentenay

Liberation and Christian Revolution in the Third World

LIBERATION THEOLOGY is not a clearly defined fixed body of doctrine. It is more like a stream with a strong, sometimes even violent, current carrying different elements along with it picked up from the land it crosses.

It belongs to history as a ship to the sea and its voyage progresses. Much more political at the beginning, with time it has become increasingly theological and spiritual, although it retains a clear awareness of the need for the liberation of the poor. Based on Christian foundations with roots in the Bible and the communities, liberation theology has developed far from the spirit of the Enlightenment, rationalism and bourgeois individualism. It has nothing to do with the French Revolution of 1789. We are in a different world. The developments which have taken place over the last twenty years confirm these observations: we are getting further and further away from 1789.

A second theology

The French Revolution is not a model for liberation theologians. Gustavo Gutierrez[1] shows how the French Revolution of 1789, which he defines as 'the experience of the possibility of a profound transformation of the existing social order', goes together with the industrial revolution 'which gives contemporary human beings a unique power and opportunity to transform nature'.[2] These two closely and mutually dependent movements offer 'a new way of being for the human person in history'. He recognises the importance of these transformations and gives the eighteenth century process its full due.

But the liberation theology movement is completely different. It does not start with 'that human minority who have the scientific and technical means as well as the political power in the world today' acquired through the two eighteenth century revolutions. 'What is at stake is not just a more rational form of economic activity or better social organisation, but through these, a matter of justice and love.'

When it reorganised society, the French Revolution did not give a voice to the poorest. It adapted to the conditions of industrial development. In the twentieth century the job to be done in dependent countries is quite different. Of course liberation theology is interested in the revolutionary process, but this is in order to promote and build a Christian revolutionary ideology. It starts from its commitment to this process and 'tries to contribute to making it more self-critical, hence more radical and global. This will happen when political commitment to liberation is set in the context of the free gift of total liberation in Jesus Christ'.[3] Becoming aware of the presence of the poor is its starting point—the desire for more justice for all. Then these feelings and this awareness must be translated into active involvement.

Short term strategies

Some of the most complex matters to unravel between revolution and liberation theology are the strategies proposed for this involvement. Let us look again at Gustavo Gutierrez' basic text: 'This discovery (of the poor, the oppressed, the exploited class) can only take place within the revolutionary struggle, which challenges the existing social order and holds that it is necessary for the people to have political power to build a truly equal and free society. This is a society in which private ownership of the means of production is abolished because it allows the minority to appropriate the fruit of the majority's labours, thereby causing the division of society into classes and the exploitation of one class by another'.[4] Lines such as these cannot hide their inspiration. A text such as the 'Christian Manifesto for Socialism' drawn up in 1972 after a meeting of Christians for socialism held in Santiago, Chile, is in the same vein. Liberation theologians speak in terms of revolutionary struggle. They have a marxist theme, at least in the '70s, their most ideological years.

But the objections to marxism have never been clarified. The tomatoes thrown at Bernard Henri Levy who had come to give a critique of marxism in Mexico say a lot about the refusal to follow Europeans in this way. Marxism remains one of the bases of analysis, even if the strictest dogmatism has disappeared.

However, important developments have taken place: on violence. Discussions on this theme have always been difficult. The tolerant discourse favoured in Europe rings false in situations of extreme tension and manifest institutional violence. The European, who shares in a world which is economically and socially dominant over Latin America, is not in a good position to speak of peace. It is from the Latin American countries that talk of peace should come. The development of an organisation like *Servicio Paz y Justicia* (SERPAJ), founded by Adolfo Perez Esquivel in 1971 and winning him the Nobel Peace Prize in 1980, is evidence of a new way of thinking. It is no longer violent revolutionary struggle which will bring about liberation, but raising the consciousness of the masses and their non-violent action. The changes which have taken place in Uruguay illustrate this process: the SERPAJ Christians were the initiators of the popular referendum demanding a revision of the policy applied to the military of the dictatorship.

The case of the Philippines is more complex. Although there is still violent guerilla warfare in which many Christians are involved, non-violence, directly inspired by the Gospel and the Church, practised by millions, drove the dictator into exile. The two strategies are opposed, causing great confusion as they claim to come from the same source. Radical change through violence is held in check by change brought about by non-violence, but no one is sure how far the latter is prepared to go.

After a period which was ideologically coloured by marxism and strategically tempted by violence, liberation theology is trying to strengthen its roots. Hence the title of a recent book by Gustavo Gutierrez, *Beber en su propio pozo en el itinerario espiritual de un pueblo*.[5] These essentially religious foundations take us further and further away from the revolutionary themes of 1789.

The poor and the people

Liberation theology's place is with human anguish and suffering. The poor are not driven by revenge, jealousy or the simple desire for power. It is a matter of life and death, their children's sickness, injustice: their poverty is the kind that kills.

The poor people themselves are central. They are the force of history, the dynamic of change. The poor preach the Gospel like Christ. The Church lives on poverty. In a recent work Christian Duquoc speaks of the way the poor determine the liberation process: 'This determination is indispensable; it marks out the actual point of unity: the identity between God and the poor'.[6]

The discovery of the poor and poverty is fundamental. It is not the poverty of the eighteenth or nineteenth century, which was linked to the incapacity of a whole economic and social system. Today democracy exists, technical means of development abound. Poverty is all the more criminal because we have all the means to overcome it. So the poor are not just the wretched who have nothing. They are exploited, crushed and despised. Their land is taken from them in Brazil. They are not given medical attention. Their children cannot go to school.

Even more seriously, as soon as Christians utter their cry for justice, they are persecuted and condemned. These catholic countries of Latin America and the Philippines have produced martyrs. In the last ten years, 200,000 people have died in the many conflicts in Central America, about one per cent of the population. In Guatemala possessing a Bible was a subversive act. Continual war and repression have hit those who worked for the liberation of these countries.

These martyrs are not forgotten. Oscar Romero is in all our hearts; like Camillo Torres but not for the same reasons. Romero was the innocent, the victim of the powers of evil. The religious dimension of martyrdom is wholly present. It inspires the action of the living, the people. Torres was a guerilla, killed in combat. He was great for his work and his courage but not for his faith.

This persecution is all the more horrible because it is perpetrated by leaders who call themselves Christians, in the name of faith and anti-communism, sometimes even with the blessing of the local church.

The next bringer of liberation is the people. The idea of the people is not the same as it was in the French Revolution. In the context of liberation theology, the individual exists in the community. Hence the importance of the base communities. The individual finds salvation in the people of God. This notion is the opposite of individualist. It is against the tradition inherited from rationalism and European liberalism, from which the French Revolution of 1789 sprang.

A popular Church, a Church of the people. Not a Church of workers, peasants or slum-dwellers. Not a Church separated from the rest of the universal Church. In this notion of the people there are no professional categories or class feelings. The people include all those who share and are interested in the fate of the poor, without exception.

There is no enemy within. The class enemy does not exist. All who want to work with the people are invited to do so, whether they be bourgeoisie or workers, foreigners or nationals. The people have no class or frontier. They welcome all who want liberation and justice. Nicaragua has put this policy into practice. Those who did not want to be part of it have had to go into exile or become the accomplices of the US, a supreme disgrace and betrayal.

Exodus and Job

So where is this terrible enemy who is identified with evil and from whom liberation must be sought? How do Latin Americans analyse their situation?

The enemy always appears external, uncontrollable, unattainable. First of all it takes the form of the liberal economic system (international capitalism etc.), to which are added the desire for profit and power, refusal of public service and the lure of corruption. Next the enemy appears in the form of the military who have played a decisive part throughout Latin America in the years 1964–79. Although they have been pushed into the background of the political scene, they are still close by and ready for action. Their return in Haiti confirms this permanent danger. Finally and above all, the enemy is North America, which manipulates the two former categories in its determination to protect its interests. Tough, unfeeling and violent Uncle Sam is omnipresent in the eyes of Latin Americans. He secretly manipulates the South American countries by means of the CIA, the mortal enemy, the incarnation of the devil.

Curiously all these enemies are linked to liberalism, the heritage of individualism. Thus liberation theology is based on the salvation and unity of the People of God, precisely the opposite to the French Revolution which discovered the individual and whose children have become the enemies of this people seeking liberation.

All these enemies in league against the poor do not leave any room for liberty. Believers are overwhelmed, become paralysed and incapable of action; they are tempted to despair. The enemy always seems stronger. It always rebounds from any crisis to crack down even harder.

The poor live their poverty in a religious way, with psalms, with the Hebrews who came out of Egypt. It is not a question of making a revolution which will overturn everything and start again at zero. Change is a process. For example, how often has the word 'process' been used to speak of the Sandinista revolution? As a religious process, it is the entry into the promised land. Of course the desire for violence is not far off. Everyone knows this and the poor know it. But the use of such means poses problems.

Christian tradition does not encourage violence. It invites us to leave this place and seek a happier land. However, it is not that easy physically just to leave. So then it speaks of the exodus as an inner exodus, a liberation process that must be undertaken. The base communities see and hear themselves and their needs in the psalms. They implore the Lord that the unrighteous should be punished and the just delivered. But this exodus cannot go on forever. One cannot always be ill-treated thus. One cannot always be the victim. One day the forces of change and liberation must prevail. One day God's victory over evil must be plain to see.

Job's meditation is not overdone. Everything seems to be in league against the victim and against the people. Gustavo Gutierrez, called one of his books *Job*.[7] One day Job will be delivered from his misfortunes. Using Job in this way raises many theological questions: God's transcendence, human suffering, the question of retribution. For Latin Americans the main point is to show the source of the poor people's inspiration and language.

A theology of the Cross

This means that there is no reason to be surprised by the place given to the Cross and the martyr in the Latin American calvary. A martyrology has been compiled.[8] It recalls all the blood already shed by the poor and those who have tried to defend them. These martyrs join Christ on the Cross.

Liberation theology develops these experiences and intuitions. It deepens such themes in essays on christology.[9] If, as Sobrino says, christology's task is to rediscover the traces of Jesus, through criticism, in our situation and within our history, clearly the Cross takes on a very particular significance when it stands above the Latin American calvary. Jesus's cross is rooted in history. It cannot be overtaken too rapidly by a Resurrection which has gone beyond all the violence and all the conflicts.

In this insistence on the Cross, liberation theology reveals its religious dimension. Following writers like Moltmann, Latin American theologians know that cross and resurrection are where Revelation takes place, of God himself and his love for humanity.

This mystery is the key to the preaching of the Gospel and its relation to the world. It should not turn Christ into a sort of heavenly person far removed from the human condition. He is the one whom all can follow in their suffering and death so that they come to share in the love that brings life beyond death.

Respect for history does not mean making it an ideological horizon emptied of a religious dimension for the sake of a shining tomorrow. But it forbids us to use Christ to escape from history.

Kairos and the Kingdom of God

So what is the relation between the present and the future? We cannot remain stuck with the image of the Cross and the symbol of Job as a prisoner to suffering. Liberation theology reflects on the kingdom of God, when love and justice will reign among human beings.

Only, for the moment, nothing changes. Conditions of life have become impossible. They have got worse over the last ten years. There is unemployment; children are not given proper education; health suffers. In Mexico, Colombia and Peru the whole social system is being destroyed from within. Corruption and violence reign supreme. In Central America, in spite of certain essentially diplomatic improvements for Nicaragua, there is still no social or political progress. And if the citizens protest, they come up against the army and the police more brutally than ever.

For certain Latin Americans the day for change seems to have come at last. Enough is enough. It is not possible to take any more. So they announce the Kairos. Gustavo Gutierrez used this term.[10] According to him Christians in Latin America are experiencing an exceptional moment of awareness, a time of solidarity and prayer, of martyrdom, which is 'a time of salvation and judgment, grace and necessity'.

Some Central Americans agree. Now the day is breaking, now we are going to reach the promised land. When we read these texts,[11] it is as if we have been taken back to the primitive Christian community: Christ's return is imminent. It is only a question of years, of months. But He is coming. In Latin America today the cup is full; revelation is at hand, God's justice is on its way. At last the poor will see daylight.

As often happens with great inspirations, the authors of this 'Kairos' feel they are opening the way for the whole world. In this, at least, they are like those who made the French Revolution: 'The oppressed majorities of the third world look towards Central America with anguish and hope'. The consequences seem obvious: 'either we close off the hope of the poor for many years to come, or we open the way prophetically to a new day for humanity and the Church'.

The concept of the Kingdom of God is central to this reflection. This is the final goal Christians must seek and which guides their action: 'Thy Kingdom come! thy will be done on earth, in Central America, as in heaven!' 'The struggle for the Kingdom': these are the last words of this recent text.

Religion and culture

In all this liberation theology we find an integration of social and religious questions. What the revolutionaries of 1789 tried to separate, in order to have a tighter grip on the political, is reunited here, not in order to create a theocratic system because the world is too secular for this, but for cultural inspiration. The base communities continually repeat that human liberation must be whole, there is no individual salvation, there is no just society without God's presence.

The liberation theologians want to maintain this link between Gospel and world, which European theology and the Latin American bourgeoisie have abandoned. Some accuse these churches of running the risk of schism. Obviously this is not a danger for populations who would abandon their faith before they abandoned the pope and the hierarchy. The most serious danger would come from individualism which is spreading like wildfire throughout Latin America as some people grow richer. This wealth carries the seeds of division and violence.

Translated by Dinah Livingstone

Notes

1. See chap. 1 of Gustavo Gutíerrez, *La Fuerza historica de los pobres* (Sigueme Press 1982). Written in 1973, this chapter summarises his main insights.
2. *Ibid.*
3. *Ibid.*
4. *Ibid.*
5. Published by Centro de Estudios y Publicaciones (CEP), Jiron Lampa 808 (Lima 1983).
6. *Libération et progressisme* (Le Cerf 1987), p. 112. Elsewhere this book also shows very well how the Enlightenment ideal of emancipation goes against liberation theology.
7. Translated into French (Le Cerf 1987).
8. DIAL.
9. *Cf.* especially Jon Sobrino's christological work *Cristología desde America Latina* and *Jesus in America Latina.*
10. In the collective work *Signos de vida y felicidad* (Lima 1983), pp. 17–22.
11. 'Karios centroamericano, el desafio a las Iglesias y al Mundo'. Duplicated 48 page text, drawn up and signed by about 100 Central American christians, dated 3 April 1988.

Contributors

PIERRE DE CHARENTENAY is a Jesuit and Doctor of Political Science. He was former Assistant Director of the Institut d'Etudes Sociales (Paris Catholic Institute); he is editor in Chief of the review *Cahiers pour croire aujourd'hui*.

GERARD CHOLVY was born in 1932. He is a professor at the Paul Valéry University at Montpellier (III). He was president of the French Association for Contemporary Religious History from 1981 to 1984. He is co-director at the National Centre for Scientific Research of the division for modern and contemporary religious history, and in charge of the section dealing with 'Christian and Jewish Youth Organisations'. His research has two main emphases: regional history (Languedoc and Roussillon, Rouergue, Vivarais) and religious history, especially *L'Eglise de France et la Révolution, Histoire régionale*, Vol. 2: *Le Midi* (Paris 1984), a general introduction to the French Church and the Revolution in the South—he is the general editor; *Mouvements de jeunesse. Chrétiens et juifs: sociabilité juvénile dans un cadre européen 1799–1968* (*Paris 1985*); with Yves-Marie Hilaire, *Histoire religieuse de la France contemporaine*, Vol. 1: 1800–1880 (Toulouse 1985); Vol. 2: 1880–1930 (Toulouse 1986); Vol. 3: 1930–1988, forthcoming; *Le patronage, ghetto ou vivier?* (Paris 1988).

PIERRE COLIN teaches philosophy and is Director of the Department of Research at the Institut Catholique in Paris. His recent articles include: 'Le kantisme dans la crise moderniste', in *Le Modernisme* (Beauchesne 1980); 'Agnosticisme et questionnement', in *Le Religieux en Occident* (Facultés Universitaires St. Louis, Brussels); 'L'enseignement républicain de la morale à la fin du XIXe siècle', in *Le Supplement*, April 1988.

JOSEPH COMBLIN was born in Brussels in 1923 and ordained in 1947. He has been in Latin America since 1958, particularly in Brazil and Chile. He is also Professor at the University of Louvain. His recent works include: *O tempo da ação* (Petrópolis 1982); *A forca da palavra* (Petrópolis 1987); *Curso breve de teologia*, 4 vols., (ed. Paul., São Paulo 1983–1986); *Antropologia cristã* (Petrópolis 1985); *Epístola aós Filipenses* 1985; *Epístola aos Colossenses* 1986; *Epístola aos Efésios* 1987; *Atos dos Apóstolos* 1988; all in the *Comentário bíblico* of Vozes, Petrópolis.

JEAN COMBY was born in Lyon (France) in 1931. He was ordained priest in the diocese of Lyon in 1959. He studied History at Lyon University and Theology at the Catholic Faculties in Lyon. He teaches Church History at the Pastoral Institute of Religious Studies and at the Lyon Theology Faculty, as well as at the Interdiocesan Seminary at Lyon. Among his publications are: *Irénée, aux origines de l'église de Lyon*, (Lyon 1977); *L'Evangile au confluent, dix-huit siècles de christianisme à Lyon*, (Lyon 1977); *Pour lire l'histoire de l'Eglise, tome 1, Des origines au XVe siècle*, (Paris 1984); *Pour lire l'histoire de l'Eglise, tome 2, Du XVe au XXe siècle*, (Paris 1986). These last two works have been translated into English, Spanish, Italian and Portuguese.

PETER EICHER was born 1943 in Winterthur (Switzerland). He studied philosophy, literature, history and theology in Freiburg (Switzerland) and Tübingen; he obtained his PhD in 1969 and Dr Theol. in 1976. Since 1977 he has been Professor of Systematic Theology (Cath.) at the University of Paderborn. He is married with five children. His main publications include: *Die anthropologische Wende* (Freiburg i.Ue. 1970); *Solidarischer Glaube* (Düsseldorf 1975); *Offenbarung—Prinzip neuzeitlicher Theologie* (Munich 1977); *Im Verborgenen offenbar* (Essen 1978); *Gottesvorstellung und Gesellschaftsentwicklung* (ed.) (Munich 1979); *Der Herr gibt's den Seinen im Schlaf* (Munich 1980); *Theologie. Eine Einführung ni das Studium* (Munich 1980); *La Théologie comme science pratique* (Paris 1982); *Das Evangelium des Friedens* (ed.) (Munich 1982); *Bürgerliche Religion, Eine theologische Kritik* (Munich 1983); *Theologie der Befreiung im Gespräch* (ed.) (Munich 1985); *Neues Handbuch theologischer Grundbegriffe* (ed.) 4 vols. (Munich 1984–85); *Karl Barth, Der reiche Jüngling* (ed.) (Munich 1986); *Der gute Widerspruch, Zum unbegriffenen Zeugnis von Karl Barth* (with M. Weinrich) (Düsseldorf, Neukirchen-Vluyn 1986).

DANIELE MENOZZI was born at Reggio Emilia, Italy in 1947. He graduated in church history at Bologna University in 1970. He is a member of the Bologna Institute of Religious Studies and has taught modern history and church history at the university there. He is now visiting professor of church history at the University of Lecce. He is editor-in-chief of the review *Cristianesimo nella storia*. He has researched the connections between Christianity and the Enlightenment (*'Philosophes' e 'Chrétiens éclairés'*, Brescia 1976) and between Christianity and the French Revolution (*Letture politiche di Gesù dall'ancien régime alla Rivoluzione*, Brescia 1980; French tr.: *Les interprétations politiques de Jésus de l'ancien régime à la révolution*, Paris 1983). Several of his publications deal with relations between Church and society ('L'église et l'histoire' in *La chrétienté en débat*, Paris 1984) and the post-conciliar period ('L'opposition au concile' in *La réception de Vatican II*, Paris 1985).

JÜRGEN MOLTMANN was born in Hamburg in 1926 and is a member of the Evangelical-Reformed Church. He studied at Göttingen, was professor at the Kirchliche Hochschule Wuppertal from 1963–67, at Bonn from 1963–67, and now holds a chair for systematic theology at Tübingen. His publications include: *Theologie der Hoffnung*, 12th ed. 1985 (ET *Theology of Hope*, 10th ed. 1983); *Perspektiven der Theologie*, 1968 (ET [selections] *Hope and Planning*, 1971); *Der Mensch*, 4th ed. 1979 (ET *Man*, 1974); *Die ersten Freigelassenen der Schöpfung*, 6th ed. 1976 (ET *Theology of Joy*, 3rd. ed. 1982 [in US as *Theology of Play*, 1972]); *Der gekreuzigte Gott*, 5th ed. 1986 (ET *The Crucified God*, 8th ed. 1985); *Kirche in der Kraft des Geistes*, 1975 (ET *The Church in the Power of the Spirit*, 2nd ed. (1981); *Zukunft der Schöpfung*, 1977 (ET *The Future of Creation*, 1979); *Trinität und Reich Gottes*, 2nd ed. 1985 (ET *The Trinity and the Kingdom of God*, 2nd ed. 1986); *Gott in der Schöpfung*, 3rd ed. 1987 (ET *God in Creation*, 1985).

CHRISTOPHER F. MOONEY, SJ, was born in 1925 in the USA and ordained in 1957. He holds a doctorate in theology from the Institut Catholique, Paris, and a doctorate in law from the University of Pennsylvania, Philadelphia. He is presently Professor of Religious Studies at Fairfield University in Connecticut and formerly Assistant Dean at the University of Pennsylvania Law School. His primary interest is the relationship between religious and legal values. His published works are *Teilhard de Chardin and the Mystery of Christ* (1966) (translated into Spanish (1967) and French (1968)); *The Making of Man* (1971); *Man Without Tears* (1975); *Religion and the American Dream* (1977); *Inequality and the American Conscience* (1982); *Public Virtue* (1986).

JEAN MOUSSÉ is a Jesuit and was born in 1921 in Nantes, France. Following his secondary studies, he decided, in 1943, to join the free French forces. Arrested at the Spanish frontier on 13 July 1943, he was a prisoner until the end of the war at Buchenwald concentration camp. He entered the Company of Jesus in 1945 and finished his studies at Münster in 1955. For three years he taught in a technical school, then in 1958 he was appointed chaplain to the *Mouvement des Cadres et Dirigeants Chrétiens* in Paris where he stayed until 1977. At present he is working at the interdisciplinary centre of the Catholic Institute in Lille, and teaches business ethics at the school of business studies in the same town (EDHEC). His publications include: *Cette liberté de violence qu'est le pouvoir* (Desclée 1982); *Le second souffle de la foi* (Luneau et Ascot, Paris 1984).

BERNARD PLONGERON was ordained priest in Paris in 1964. He taught at the universities of Strasbourg and Louvain and is now Professor of Letters and Theology at the Institut Catholique in Paris. He is a member of the national committee of the CNRS and since 1985 has been head of the research group on modern and contemporary religious history. He holds a diploma from the Institut d'Etudes Politiques in Paris and *doctorat d'état* in both history and theology. Fr Plongeron has published 60 books and articles on the relations between religious attitudes and politics in Europe in the eighteenth and nineteenth centuries, most recently a revised edition of *La vie quotidienne du clergé français au XVIIIe siècle* (Paris 1988, 1st edn. 1974). He is also on the editorial boards of many journals, including, *Revue de l'Histoire de l'Eglise en France, Studies in Religion/Sciences Religieuses* (Canada) and *Annals of Scholarship* (New York).

BERNARD QUELQUEJEU was born in Paris in 1932 and entered the Dominican Order in 1955. He is professor of Anthropology and Philosophical Ethics at the Institut Catholique in Paris and editor of the *Revue des Sciences philosophiques et théologiques*. His numerous publications on moral philosophy and politics include (in collaboration) *Vers une éthique politique: l'éthique face à l'ingouvernabilité de l'homme* (Paris 1987). He was a contributor to *Le Manifeste de la liberté chrétienne* (Paris 1976).

SUBSCRIBE TO CONCILIUM

'**CONCILIUM** a journal of world standing, is far and away the best.'
The Times

'... it is certainly the most variegated and stimulating school of theology active today. **CONCILIUM** ought to be available to all clergy and layfolk who are anxious to keep abreast of what is going on in the theological workshops of the world today.'
Theology

CONCILIUM is published on the first of every alternate month beginning in February. Over twelve issues (two years), themes are drawn from the following key areas: dogma, liturgy, pastoral theology, ecumenism, moral theology, the sociology of religion, Church history, canon law, spirituality, scripture, Third World theology and Feminist theology (see back cover for details of 1988 titles). As a single issue sells for £5.45 a subscription can mean savings of up to £12.75.

SUBSCRIPTION RATES 1988

	UK	USA	Canada	Other Countries
New Subscribers	£19.95	$39.95	$49.95	£19.95
Regular Subscribers	£27.50	$49.95	$59.95	£27.50
Airmail		$65.00	$79.95	£37.50

All prices include postage and packing. **CONCILIUM** is sent 'accelerated surface post' to the USA and Canada and by surface mail to other destinations.

Cheques payable to T & T Clark. Personal cheques in $ currency acceptable. Credit card payments by *Access*, *Mastercard* and *Visa*.

'A bold and confident venture in contemporary theology. All the best new theologians are contributing to this collective summa'.
Commonweal

Send your order direct to the Publishers

T & T CLARK LTD

Publishers   *since 1821*

59 GEORGE STREET
EDINBURGH
EH2 2LQ
SCOTLAND

CONCILIUM

8. **Polarization in the Church.** Ed. Hans Küng and Walter Kasper. 0 8164 2572 8 156pp.

9. **Spiritual Revivals.** Ed. Christian Duquoc and Casiano Floristán. 0 8164 2573 6 156pp.

0. **Power and the Word of God.** Ed. Franz Bockle and Jacques Marie Pohier. 0 8164 2574 4 156pp.

1. **The Church as Institution.** Ed. Gregory Baum and Andrew Greeley. 0 8164 2575 2 168pp.

2. **Politics and Liturgy.** Ed. Herman Schmidt and David Power. 0 8164 2576 0 156pp.

3. **Jesus Christ and Human Freedom.** Ed. Edward Schillebeeckx and Bas van Iersel. 0 8164 2577 9 168pp.

4. **The Experience of Dying.** Ed. Norbert Greinacher and Alois Müller. 0 8164 2578 7 156pp.

5. **Theology of Joy.** Ed. Johannes Baptist Metz and Jean-Pierre Jossua. 0 8164 2579 5 164pp.

6. **The Mystical and Political Dimension of the Christian Faith.** Ed. Claude Geffré and Gustavo Guttierez. 0 8164 2580 9 168pp.

7. **The Future of the Religious Life.** Ed. Peter Huizing and William Bassett. 0 8164 2094 7 96pp.

8. **Christians and Jews.** Ed. Hans Küng and Walter Kasper. 0 8164 2095 5 96pp.

9. **Experience of the Spirit.** Ed. Peter Huizing and William Bassett. 0 8164 2096 3 144pp.

0. **Sexuality in Contemporary Catholicism.** Ed. Franz Bockle and Jacques Marie Pohier. 0 8164 2097 1 126pp.

1. **Ethnicity.** Ed. Andrew Greeley and Gregory Baum. 0 8164 2145 5 120pp.

2. **Liturgy and Cultural Religious Traditions.** Ed. Herman Schmidt and David Power. 0 8164 2146 2 120pp.

3. **A Personal God?** Ed. Edward Schillebeeckx and Bas van Iersel. 0 8164 2149 8 142pp.

4. **The Poor and the Church.** Ed. Norbert Greinacher and Alois Müller. 0 8164 2147 1 128pp.

5. **Christianity and Socialism.** Ed. Johannes Baptist Metz and Jean-Pierre Jossua. 0 8164 2148 X 144pp.

6. **The Churches of Africa: Future Prospects.** Ed. Claude Geffré and Bertrand Luneau. 0 8164 2150 1 128pp.

7. **Judgement in the Church.** Ed. William Bassett and Peter Huizing. 0 8164 2166 8 128pp.

8. **Why Did God Make Me?** Ed. Hans Küng and Jürgen Moltmann. 0 8164 2167 6 112pp.

9. **Charisms in the Church.** Ed. Christian Duquoc and Casiano Floristán. 0 8164 2168 4 128pp.

0. **Moral Formation and Christianity.** Ed. Franz Bockle and Jacques Marie Pohier. 0 8164 2169 2 120pp.

1. **Communication in the Church.** Ed. Gregory Baum and Andrew Greeley. 0 8164 2170 6 126pp.

112. **Liturgy and Human Passage.** Ed. David Power and Luis Maldonado. 0 8164 2608 2 136pp.

113. **Revelation and Experience.** Ed. Edward Schillebeeckx and Bas van Iersel. 0 8164 2609 0 134pp.

114. **Evangelization in the World Today.** Ed. Norbert Greinacher and Alois Müller. 0 8164 2610 4 136pp.

115. **Doing Theology in New Places.** Ed. Jean-Pierre Jossua and Johannes Baptist Metz. 0 8164 2611 2 120pp.

116. **Buddhism and Christianity.** Ed. Claude Geffré and Mariasusai Dhavamony. 0 8164 2612 0 136pp.

117. **The Finances of the Church.** Ed. William Bassett and Peter Huizing. 0 8164 2197 8 160pp.

118. **An Ecumenical Confession of Faith?** Ed. Hans Küng and Jürgen Moltmann. 0 8164 2198 6 136pp.

119. **Discernment of the Spirit and of Spirits.** Ed. Casiano Floristán and Christian Duquoc. 0 8164 2199 4 136pp.

120. **The Death Penalty and Torture.** Ed. Franz Bockle and Jacques Marie Pohier. 0 8164 2200 1 136pp.

121. **The Family in Crisis or in Transition.** Ed. Andrew Greeley. 0 567 30001 3 128pp.

122. **Structures of Initiation in Crisis.** Ed. Luis Maldonado and David Power. 0 567 30002 1 128pp.

123. **Heaven.** Ed. Bas van Iersel and Edward Schillebeeckx. 0 567 30003 X 120pp.

124. **The Church and the Rights of Man.** Ed. Alois Müller and Norbert Greinacher. 0 567 30004 8 140pp.

125. **Christianity and the Bourgeoisie.** Ed. Johannes Baptist Metz. 0 567 30005 6 144pp.

126. **China as a Challenge to the Church.** Ed. Claude Geffré and Joseph Spae. 0 567 30006 4 136pp.

127. **The Roman Curia and the Communion of Churches.** Ed. Peter Huizing and Knut Walf. 0 567 30007 2 144pp.

128. **Conflicts about the Holy Spirit.** Ed. Hans Küng and Jürgen Moltmann. 0 567 30008 0 144pp.

129. **Models of Holiness.** Ed. Christian Duquoc and Casiano Floristán. 0 567 30009 9 128pp.

130. **The Dignity of the Despised of the Earth.** Ed. Jacques Marie Pohier and Dietmar Mieth. 0 567 30010 2 144pp.

131. **Work and Religion.** Ed. Gregory Baum. 0 567 30011 0 148pp.

132. **Symbol and Art in Worship.** Ed. Luis Maldonado and David Power. 0 567 30012 9 136pp.

133. **Right of the Community to a Priest.** Ed. Edward Schillebeeckx and Johannes Baptist Metz. 0 567 30013 7 142pp.

134. **Women in a Men's Church.** Ed. Virgil Elizondo and Norbert Greinacher. 0 567 30014 5 144pp.

135. **True and False Universality of Christianity.** Ed. Claude Geffré and Jean-Pierre Jossua. 0 567 30015 3 138pp.

136. **What is Religion? An Inquiry for Christian Theology.** Ed. Mircea Eliade and David Tracy. 0 567 30016 1 98pp.

137. **Electing our Own Bishops.** Ed. Peter Huizing and Knut Walf. 0 567 30017 X 112pp.

138. **Conflicting Ways of Interpreting the Bible.** Ed. Hans Küng and Jürgen Moltmann. 0 567 30018 8 112pp.

139. **Christian Obedience.** Ed. Casiano Floristán and Christian Duquoc. 0 567 30019 6 96pp.

140. **Christian Ethics and Economics: the North-South Conflict.** Ed. Dietmar Mieth and Jacques Marie Pohier. 0 567 30020 X 128pp.

141. **Neo-Conservatism: Social and Religious Phenomenon.** Ed. Gregory Baum and John Coleman. 0 567 30021 8.

142. **The Times of Celebration.** Ed. David Power and Mary Collins. 0 567 30022 6.

143. **God as Father.** Ed. Edward Schillebeeckx and Johannes Baptist Metz. 0 567 30023 4.

144. **Tensions Between the Churches of the First World and the Third World.** Ed. Virgil Elizondo and Norbert Greinacher. 0 567 30024 2.

145. **Nietzsche and Christianity.** Ed. Claude Geffré and Jean-Pierre Jossua. 0 567 30025 0.

146. **Where Does the Church Stand?** Ed. Giuseppe Alberigo. 0 567 30026 9.

147. **The Revised Code of Canon Law: a Missed Opportunity?** Ed. Peter Huizing and Knut Walf. 0 567 30027 7.

148. **Who Has the Say in the Church?** Ed. Hans Küng and Jürgen Moltmann. 0 567 30028 5.

149. **Francis of Assisi Today.** Ed. Casiano Floristán and Christian Duquoc. 0 567 30029 3.

150. **Christian Ethics: Uniformity, Universality, Pluralism.** Ed. Jacques Pohier and Dietmar Mieth. 0 567 30030 7.

151. **The Church and Racism.** Ed. Gregory Baum and John Coleman. 0 567 30031 5.

152. **Can we always celebrate the Eucharist?** Ed. Mary Collins and David Power. 0 567 30032 3.

153. **Jesus, Son of God?** Ed. Edward Schillebeeckx and Johannes-Baptist Metz. 0 567 30033 1.

154. **Religion and Churches in Eastern Europe.** Ed. Virgil ELizondo and Norbert Greinacher. 0 567 30034 X.

155. **'The Human', Criterion of Christian Existence?** Ed. Claude Geffré and Jean-Pierre Jossua. 0 567 30035 8.

156. **The Challenge of Psychology to Faith.** Ed. Steven Kepnes (Guest Editor) and David Tracy. 0 567 30036 6.

157. **May Church Ministers be Politicians?** Ed. Peter Huizing and Knut Walf. 0 567 30037 4.

158. **The Right to Dissent.** Ed. Hans Küng and Jürgen Moltmann. 0 567 30038 2.

CONCILIUM

CONCILIUM 1988

All back issues are still in print: available from bookshops (price £5.95) or direct from the publishers (£6.45/US$10.95/Can$12.75 including postage and packing).

T & T CLARK LTD, 59 GEORGE STREET, EDINBURGH EH2 2LQ, SCOTLAND